Trust, Taxes, and Wills Bundle: Retirement & Estate Planning Book

Golden Folio Editions

Table of contents

From Overwhelmed to Organized

Marilyn found the will in a fireproof box in the hall closet, exactly where her husband Tom said it would be. It had cost them three hundred dollars from a storefront lawyer eleven years earlier, and it named her as executor, left everything to her, and named their son as backup if anything happened to them both. She read it twice, made copies, and felt, for about a week, like the hard part was behind her.

Then she called Tom's 401(k) provider to start the paperwork, and a representative on the other end asked her to confirm her name against the account. It didn't match. The beneficiary on file was Tom's first wife, a marriage that had ended nineteen years before he and Marilyn ever met. Nobody had updated the form. Not when they married, not when their son was born, not when Tom changed jobs twice and rolled the account over each time, carrying the same outdated instruction forward without anyone noticing. The will said one thing. The account said another. And under federal law, the account wins. The will, the three hundred dollars, the eleven years of assuming the matter was settled — none of it mattered. Tom's retirement savings, which made up more than half of everything he owned, went to a woman he hadn't spoken to in two decades.

This is not a story about carelessness. Tom was not a careless man. He paid his bills on time, kept his car serviced, and did the responsible thing by getting a will made while his son was still small. What he didn't know — what almost nobody knows until it costs them — is that a will is only one document in a set of four, and the other three don't automatically follow its lead. A will directs certain assets through probate. A trust, if one exists, operates under entirely separate instructions. Powers of attorney and healthcare directives govern what happens if you're alive but unable to act. And beneficiary designations — the forms buried in retirement accounts, life insurance policies, and payable-on-death bank accounts — override the will completely for the assets they cover, no matter what the will says or how recently it was signed.

The real threat to your family isn't death, and despite what the tax-planning industry might have you believe, for the overwhelming majority of households it isn't the IRS either. The threat is contradiction. It's four systems that were each set up at different times, by different processes, sometimes by different professionals who never spoke to one another, all quietly assuming they were the ones in charge. Most people don't discover the conflict until someone is grieving and trying to settle an estate at the same time, which is the worst possible moment to learn that the paperwork doesn't agree with itself.

Here is the thesis this entire book is built on, stated plainly so there's no confusion about what you're holding: an estate plan is not a document. It is four coordinated systems — your will, your trust if you have or need one, your incapacity documents, and your beneficiary designations and account titling — and they have to say the same thing. Get all four aligned, and your family settles your affairs in a matter of weeks, largely on their own, at a cost you decided on in advance. Leave even one out of step with the others, and you've built exactly the kind of trap Marilyn walked into, regardless of how much you spent on legal advice or how recently you updated anything.

The deal this book is offering you is specific, and it's worth being upfront about both sides of it. Worked through in order, chapter by chapter, task by task, this book will take you from wherever your planning currently stands to a signed, funded, internally consistent estate plan within ninety days — or, if your situation calls for professional drafting, to a precise, organized brief you can hand an attorney so that meeting costs you an hour instead of four. That's the promise. It comes with a limit stated just as plainly: estate law varies by state, sometimes significantly, and this book is not a substitute for an attorney licensed where you live. What it will do is tell you exactly which decisions are yours to make, which ones need a professional's signature, and how to walk into that professional's office already knowing what you need — which is where most of the wasted time and money in this process actually happens.

The path through the book follows the logic of the problem itself. You'll start by diagnosing where you currently stand and building a complete inventory of what you own and how it's titled, because you cannot fix contradictions you haven't found. From there, the chapters move through each of the four systems in turn — wills, trusts, incapacity planning, and beneficiary designations — before turning to the tax questions that trip up retirement accounts and larger estates, and finally to the complications that don't fit the standard template: blended families, family businesses, disagreements among heirs. Four recurring elements will show up throughout: a Plain English box that translates the legal terminology as it appears, a Case File built from a real pattern of what goes wrong, a Cost Check that tells you what to expect to pay before you commit to anything, and an Action Step that turns each chapter into something done rather than something merely read.

You don't need to read straight through. Chapters one and two are the foundation and should be read in order — they build the diagnostic tool and the inventory that everything else depends on. After that, a short self-assessment at the end of chapter one will score your situation and point you toward the specific chapters that matter most for your circumstances, so you can skip what doesn't apply and spend your time where the real risk sits. This isn't a book meant to be read cover to cover out of obligation. It's a tool meant to get four documents to finally agree with each other, and to get you there faster than Marilyn ever got the chance to.

Chapter 1 — The Hidden Cost of No Plan

Numbers convince people who stories don't. So before this book asks you to do anything, it's worth putting an actual price tag on the thing you're currently carrying around unexamined: the cost of leaving your affairs the way they are right now.

Start with probate, because it's the piece most people underestimate by the widest margin. Probate is the court process that validates a will, appoints an executor with legal authority, and supervises the transfer of assets to heirs. It is not optional in most cases, and it is rarely fast. Depending on the state, the size of the estate, and whether anyone contests anything, a straightforward probate can run anywhere from several months to well over a year, and the fees attached to it — court costs, executor commissions, attorney fees, appraisal costs — are typically calculated as a percentage of the estate's value rather than a flat rate. In some states that percentage is set by statute; in others it's negotiated, which sounds better until you realize negotiation happens after your family is already grieving and has little leverage or appetite for the fight. The exact figures shift by jurisdiction and change over time, so treat any specific number you hear as a starting point to verify against your own state's current probate code, not as a fact to bank on. What doesn't shift much is the shape of the problem: the larger and more complicated the estate, the more expensive and slower the process becomes, and none of that expense buys your family anything they wanted.

Then there's the cost that almost nobody prices in advance, because it only shows up if you're unlucky: court-appointed guardianship. Estate planning conversations tend to focus entirely on death, but incapacity — a stroke, an accident, the slow onset of dementia — arrives first far more often than people expect, and it arrives without warning. If you become unable to manage your own affairs and haven't legally named someone to step in for you, your family doesn't get to simply take over. They have to petition a court to be appointed your guardian or conservator, a process that involves medical evaluations, hearings, attorney fees on both sides in some cases, and ongoing court supervision of every decision made on your behalf afterward. It is slower than most families expect, it is public record, and it can pit siblings against each other if more than one person believes they should be the one in charge. A properly executed power of attorney, which chapter five will walk you through, generally avoids this entire process for a fraction of the cost and almost none of the delay. Skipping it doesn't save money. It just moves the expense to a moment when your family has the least capacity to absorb it.

Illiquid assets create a different kind of damage, one measured less in dollars and more in forced decisions made under pressure. A house, a small business, a piece of land, a collection built over decades — none of these convert to cash quickly, and estate settlement often runs on a clock, whether that clock is set by a mortgage payment that still needs to be made, a tax bill coming due, or simply the practical need to divide value among several heirs who can't all live in the same house. Families without a plan frequently end up selling these assets faster and cheaper than they would have chosen to under normal circumstances, not because the market forced it, but because the timeline did. The business that took your father thirty years to build gets sold to the first reasonable offer within eighteen months, because nobody had a plan for who would run it or how the other siblings would get their share without a sale.

And then there's the damage that doesn't show up in any account statement: what disorganized planning does to the people left behind. Ambiguous instructions, unequal treatment that was never explained, and assets that quietly contradict each other are the standard ingredients of estate litigation between siblings, and that litigation rarely stays contained to the courtroom. Families that functioned fine for decades can fracture permanently over a dispute that a clearly written, properly aligned set of documents would have prevented entirely. Legal fees in a contested estate can run into tens of thousands of dollars, paid out of the estate itself, which means every dollar spent fighting is a dollar that doesn't reach anyone. But the number that matters more, and the one no dollar figure captures, is the relationship that doesn't survive the fight.

Put those four categories together — probate costs and delay, guardianship risk, forced sales of assets that deserved better timing, and the very real possibility of family conflict — and you have a rough shape of what "no plan" actually costs. It isn't zero, and it isn't abstract. It's a number sitting quietly in your file drawer right now, waiting for a moment you don't get to choose. The rest of this chapter, and the audit at the end of it, will help you estimate your own.

1.2 The Four Ways a Plan Fails

There are only four ways an estate plan actually falls apart, and it's worth naming all four clearly, because two of them are far more common — and far more expensive — than most people assume.

The first is the simplest: no documents exist at all. No will, no trust, no power of attorney, nothing filed anywhere. This is the failure mode people picture when they think about not having a plan, and it's genuinely serious — it means your state's default inheritance laws decide who gets what, a court appoints your executor rather than you choosing one, and if you have minor children, a judge decides who raises them rather than you naming a guardian yourself. But this failure mode has one advantage the other three don't: it's honest. Nobody with no documents believes they're protected. The danger is visible, which means it's usually the first thing people fix once they understand the stakes.

The second failure mode is quieter and considerably more dangerous, because it hides behind the comfort of having done something once. Stale documents are ones that were accurate the day they were signed and have simply never been touched since — sometimes for five years, sometimes for twenty. A will written before a second marriage. A guardian named for children who are now adults with families of their own. An executor who has since passed away, moved out of state, or simply isn't the right choice anymore given how the family has changed. The document still exists, still looks official, and will still be accepted by a court — but it may no longer reflect anything close to what you'd actually want, and nobody finds out until it's being read aloud after the fact.

The third failure mode is the one that quietly wrecked things for the widow in this book's introduction: an unfunded trust. This happens when someone does the work of creating a revocable living trust — often paying a meaningful legal fee to have it drafted correctly — and then never completes the second, less glamorous half of the process, which is retitling their actual assets into the trust's name. A trust that doesn't hold any assets provides none of the protection it was built for. The house is still titled in your name personally. The brokerage account never got the paperwork updated. The trust sits in a drawer as a beautifully drafted document that legally owns nothing, while everything you actually meant to protect still runs straight through probate, exactly as if the trust had never been created. This is, without much competition, the most expensive failure on this list relative to what people paid to avoid it.

The fourth failure mode is contradictory beneficiary forms, and it's the one this book returns to again and again because it is both the most common and the most avoidable. Retirement accounts, life insurance policies, and payable-on-death bank accounts all transfer according to whatever beneficiary form is on file with the institution that holds them — completely independent of what your will says, no matter how recently the will was updated or how clearly it states your intentions. An ex-spouse never removed from a 401(k) form, a beneficiary line left blank so the account defaults to probate anyway, a child named without a contingent beneficiary in case that child predeceases you — these small, easily overlooked details override an otherwise perfectly good will, every time.

Here's the detail worth sitting with: the two most expensive failures on this list — the unfunded trust and the contradictory beneficiary form — happen almost exclusively to people who already paid for professional estate planning. They are not failures of neglect. They are failures of an incomplete process, one that stopped at the signature instead of continuing through to the paperwork that actually moves assets. Which means the sentence "I have a will" or even "I have a trust" is not a fact. It's a claim, and like any claim, it's only worth something once it's been checked.

1.3 Score Your Own Risk

The audit below takes about ten minutes and gives you an honest answer to the question this chapter has been building toward: which failure mode, if any, applies to you. Answer each item yes or no as it genuinely stands today, not as you intend it to stand, and not based on what you remember signing years ago. If you're not certain of an answer, treat that uncertainty itself as a no — it means the item needs verification, which is exactly what this audit is designed to surface.

Question one: do you have a signed will. Question two: has it been reviewed or updated within the last five years. Question three: does it still name people you'd currently choose as executor and, if relevant, as guardian for minor children. Question four: if you have a revocable living trust, has every major asset — your home, your bank and brokerage accounts, any business interest — actually been retitled into the trust's name. Question five: do you have a durable power of attorney for financial matters that is current and would be honored by your bank today. Question six: do you have a healthcare directive and a named healthcare proxy.

Question seven: have you personally confirmed, within the past year, who is listed as beneficiary on every retirement account you hold. Question eight: the same question for every life insurance policy you own. Question nine: does every account with a beneficiary designation also have a contingent beneficiary named, in case your first choice predeceases you. Question ten: if you've divorced, remarried, had a child, or lost a spouse since your documents were last signed, have your documents been updated to reflect it. Question eleven: does anyone in your family know where your original signed documents are physically located. Question twelve: if you own property in more than one state, or hold a business interest, have those specific assets been addressed by name in your planning.

Count your no answers, including any you marked as uncertain. Zero to two puts you in the green zone — your foundation is largely sound, and you should move through this book selectively, focusing on chapters four through nine, where the more advanced strategies live. Three to six puts you in amber — you have real gaps, but they're fixable, and chapters two through six should be your priority, in order, over the coming weeks. Seven or more puts you in red, and it means the core of your plan needs rebuilding from the ground up, starting with chapter two's inventory process and moving straight through the book in sequence rather than skipping ahead.

Whatever zone you land in, put a date on it now, not later. Green zone: pick one weekend within the next thirty days to complete the beneficiary verification in chapter six. Amber zone: give yourself sixty days to work through the priority chapters and reach a fully aligned plan. Red zone: ninety days, starting today, following the book in order — which happens to be exactly the promise this book made you in the introduction. A risk score without a deadline is just a piece of trivia about yourself. The date is what turns it into a plan.

Chapter 2 — Map Your Estate Before You Plan

Before you write a single new document, before you call an attorney, before you decide whether you need a trust or just a will, you need one page that doesn't exist yet in most households: a complete, honest picture of what you actually own, how each piece is legally titled, and who is named on it right now. Call it the Estate Map. It's the single most useful page in this entire book, and every chapter that follows assumes you've built it.

The reason this comes before anything else is not procedural tidiness. It's that most people planning their estate are working from a picture in their head that doesn't match the paperwork in their file drawer, and the gap between those two things is exactly where the expensive failures from chapter one live. You cannot fix a contradiction you haven't found, and you cannot find it by thinking hard about your finances. You find it by writing down, asset by asset, three separate pieces of information that almost nobody keeps in one place: what the asset is, how it's currently titled, and who's named on it.

Start with the first column — what you own. This means everything, not just the obvious large items. Your home, obviously, and any other real estate, including a vacation property or land you inherited and never quite dealt with. Every bank account, checking and savings, at every institution, because most people have more of these scattered around than they remember. Every retirement account — 401(k), traditional IRA, Roth IRA, pension — from every employer you've ever had, including the old 401(k) sitting untouched from a job you left fifteen years ago. Every brokerage or investment account. Life insurance policies, including any small ones provided through an employer that people tend to forget entirely. Any interest in a business, even a small one, even one you think of as more of a hobby than a company. Vehicles, if they carry meaningful value. And increasingly, a category people still routinely leave off entirely: digital assets, meaning anything from cryptocurrency to accumulated loyalty program balances to accounts that hold real monetary value but exist only online. List all of it. This first pass will likely be longer than you expect, and that's the point — the goal here is completeness, not tidiness.

The second column is where the real work happens, because it asks a question most people have never actually answered about their own property: how is this titled. Titling is the legal ownership structure attached to an asset, and it matters more than almost anything else in this book, for reasons the rest of this section will explain. A house might be titled in your name alone, in joint tenancy with a spouse, as tenants in common with a sibling from an inheritance, or inside a trust if you've already set one up. A bank account might be titled individually, jointly with a right of survivorship, or as payable-on-death to a named person. For each asset in your first column, write down exactly how it's currently titled — and if you don't know, that uncertainty itself is information worth recording, because it tells you exactly where to start making calls.

The third column asks who's named. For any account with a beneficiary designation — retirement accounts, life insurance, payable-on-death and transfer-on-death accounts — write down exactly who is listed as primary beneficiary, and who, if anyone, is listed as contingent. Not who you think is listed. Not who you meant to list. Who is actually on file with the institution right now, verified if possible rather than remembered.

Here is the mechanic this entire book is built around, and it's worth stating as plainly as language allows: for most people, the will controls a minority of what they own. Retirement accounts pass according to their beneficiary form. Jointly titled property passes automatically to the surviving co-owner, outside of probate entirely, regardless of what any will says. Payable-on-death and transfer-on-death accounts bypass the will completely by design. Life insurance goes to whoever is named on the policy. What's left for the will to actually govern is typically whatever's left over — assets titled solely in your name with no beneficiary designation attached, which for many households turns out to be a smaller slice than they assumed. People spend real money getting a will carefully drafted and then feel protected, without realizing that the document they invested in only has authority over a portion of their estate, sometimes a modest portion, while the larger share is being silently directed by forms filled out years earlier at a bank counter or an HR onboarding session, often without much thought at the time.

This is why the Estate Map has to come first. Once you can see, asset by asset, what's actually titled where and who's actually named on each account, you're no longer planning in the abstract. You're looking at the real mechanism that will move your wealth when the time comes, and you can start asking the only question that matters going forward: does this match what I actually want. The next section will show you how to sort every line on this page into the two categories that determine which parts of your plan need attention first — and how little of what you own may currently be running through the document you thought was in charge.

2.2 Probate or Not: Marking Every Line

Take the Estate Map you just built and add one more column to it, a simple two-letter marker: P for probate, NP for non-probate. This single step will do more to clarify your actual situation than almost anything else in this book, because it turns an abstract worry about "having a plan" into a concrete, visual fact about exactly how much of what you own is currently under your will's control and how much isn't.

The rule for marking each line is straightforward once you understand what it's actually testing. An asset is non-probate if it transfers automatically to someone else by operation of law or by contract, without needing a court to authorize the transfer. An asset is probate if, in the absence of some other mechanism, it has to pass through the court process to be legally transferred to whoever inherits it. Go down your list and apply this test to each item honestly, based on the titling and beneficiary information you already recorded, not on assumptions.

Retirement accounts with a named beneficiary are non-probate — they pass directly to that person by contract with the plan administrator. Life insurance with a named beneficiary works the same way. Bank accounts titled as payable-on-death, or brokerage accounts titled as transfer-on-death, are non-probate for the same reason. Property held in joint tenancy with right of survivorship, common for married couples, is non-probate — it passes automatically and immediately to the surviving owner the moment the other dies, with no court involvement at all. And any asset that's been properly retitled into a funded trust is non-probate, because the trust, not you personally, is the legal owner, and the trust simply continues operating under its own instructions.

Everything else is probate. A house titled in your name alone. A bank account with no payable-on-death designation. A car. Personal property — furniture, jewelry, art, the contents of a home. A retirement account, unusually, that lists no living beneficiary or lists "my estate" as the beneficiary, which pulls it back into probate despite being the kind of account people assume avoids it. Anything titled solely in your name that isn't otherwise covered by a beneficiary form or joint ownership defaults to this category.

Now look at the categories people consistently forget to include at all, because they're either newer than most estate planning habits or simply don't feel like "estate" items until someone points them out. Digital assets are a growing and genuinely underestimated one — cryptocurrency held in a personal wallet, for instance, has no beneficiary form and no joint owner unless you've deliberately arranged one, which typically makes it probate property, and worse, property that can become permanently inaccessible if nobody else knows the access credentials exist. Accumulated loyalty points and airline miles sit in a strange in-between category; many programs have their own transfer rules entirely separate from probate law, and some simply expire on death regardless of what your will says, which means the only real protection is knowing the specific program's policy in advance. An interest in an LLC or small business is probate property unless the operating agreement itself specifies a different transfer mechanism, and even then, that agreement's terms typically override anything your will attempts to say about it — a detail chapter nine covers in more depth. And property in a second state, a lake house or a hunting cabin held in your name alone, doesn't just sit in your regular probate estate. It typically triggers a second, entirely separate probate proceeding in whatever state the property is located, run under that state's rules, adding real time and real cost on top of whatever your home state's process already involves.

Once every line is marked, sit back and look at the full page. For most people going through this exercise for the first time, the result is genuinely surprising: the probate column, the one governed by the will, often turns out to be smaller than expected, sometimes covering only the house and a handful of personal items, while the larger share of actual wealth is already flowing through beneficiary forms and joint titling that nobody thought to review in years. This is the moment the abstract idea from section 2.1 becomes personal and specific. You're not reading about how wills work in general anymore. You're looking at your own numbers, sorted honestly, showing you exactly where your real leverage sits.

2.3 Deciding What You Actually Want

With the map built and every asset sorted, there's a temptation to move straight into tools — should you get a trust, how should the will be worded, which forms need updating. Resist it for one more step. Before you choose any instrument, you need to write down, in plain language, what you actually want to happen, because every decision in the rest of this book will be tested against that statement, and skipping it means building a plan around structure instead of intent.

Start with who receives what. Not in legal language, just honestly: does everything split evenly among your children, or does one of them need more support than the others for a real reason — a disability, a difference in financial stability, care they provided you that the others didn't. Is there a specific asset, the house or a piece of property, that you want to go to a particular person rather than being sold and divided. Are there people outside your immediate family, a sibling, a friend, a charity, who should receive something specific.

Next, think about timing and conditions, because "receives what" is only half the question. A twenty-two-year-old inheriting a large sum outright is a very different outcome than a fifty-year-old inheriting the same amount, and plenty of parents who'd happily leave money to an adult child feel very differently about that child receiving it all at once at twenty-five. Do you want distributions staggered by age. Do you want funds held back until a specific milestone — finishing college, reaching a certain age, demonstrating some measure of stability. None of this needs to be legally precise yet. It needs to be honest.

Finally, and this is the part most people skip past too quickly, decide who actually holds the reins, because a plan is only as good as the people responsible for carrying it out. There are four fiduciary roles worth understanding clearly at this stage, even before you've decided which documents you need. An executor administers your will and settles your probate estate. A trustee manages a trust's assets according to its terms, potentially for years if the trust holds funds back for young beneficiaries. A financial agent acts under your power of attorney if you become incapacitated, managing your finances while you're alive but unable to. A guardian raises your minor children if both parents are gone. These roles don't need to go to the same person, and in many families, they shouldn't.

The instinct most people follow is to default to birth order or perceived closeness — the oldest child, the one who calls the most, the one who'd be hurt if they weren't picked. Resist that instinct in favor of a better rubric: who is actually organized enough to handle deadlines and paperwork under pressure, who is level-headed enough to manage money responsibly and not personally, who lives close enough or is willing enough to handle the practical logistics, and who can be trusted not to let old sibling dynamics affect decisions that need to be fair. The person best suited to raise your children is not automatically the person best suited to manage a trust for them, and naming the same person for every role because it feels simpler often creates the exact kind of strain a good plan is supposed to prevent.

Now put it together. Write one paragraph, in your own words, that states who receives what, under what conditions, and who you trust to make it happen. Keep it short enough to reread in under a minute. This is your Distribution Intent statement, and its purpose isn't to be legally binding — it won't be, on its own. Its purpose is to become the test you run every later decision through. When chapter three asks you to choose an executor, or chapter four asks whether a trust makes sense for your situation, or chapter nine asks how to structure things for a blended family, you'll come back to this paragraph and ask the only question that actually matters: does this choice serve what I just wrote down. Everything from here forward is really just the mechanics of making that one paragraph true.

Chapter 3 — Write a Will That Actually Works

By now you've built the Estate Map, sorted every asset into probate or non-probate, and written a Distribution Intent statement that says, in your own words, who gets what and who's in charge of making it happen. This chapter turns that intent into the first real legal instrument: the will. But before walking through how to write one well, it's worth being precise about what a will actually does, because the confusion around this single document causes more misplaced confidence than almost anything else in estate planning. A will is powerful within its lane. It is also, for most people, a smaller piece of the overall plan than they assume, and understanding exactly where its authority starts and stops is what separates a plan that works from one that quietly fails the way Tom's did in the introduction.

Start with what a will genuinely accomplishes, because it does three real things, and each one matters.

First, a will names your executor — the person legally responsible for administering your estate after you die. This is not a symbolic title. The executor is the one who files the will with the probate court, notifies creditors, pays any outstanding debts and taxes owed by the estate, inventories the probate assets, and ultimately distributes what remains according to the will's instructions. Without a will, a court appoints someone to fill this role using its own default priority list, usually starting with a surviving spouse and moving through family members in order, regardless of whether that person is the one you'd actually choose, or the one best equipped to handle it. Naming your own executor is one of the will's most direct and consequential functions, because it puts the decision in your hands instead of a judge's.

Second, if you have minor children, a will nominates their guardian. This is arguably the single most important function a will performs for parents of young children, and it's one that no other document in your planning toolkit replicates. If both parents die or become unable to care for a child and no guardian has been named, a court decides who raises that child, based on whatever evidence and testimony is presented at the time — which might include family members you'd never have chosen, disagreeing with each other in a courtroom about who should get custody. A will lets you make that decision yourself, in advance, while you're in a position to think clearly about it rather than leaving it to be litigated during the worst moment of your family's life. Even people with very few assets and no real need for complex estate planning should have a will for this reason alone if they have minor children.

Third, and this is where chapter two's work connects directly to this one, a will directs your probate assets — specifically, and only, the assets you marked with a P on your Estate Map. This is the residuary and specific-bequest function most people picture when they think about a will: your house, if titled solely in your name, your personal property, any account with no beneficiary designation or joint owner attached. The will tells the executor and the court how these specific assets should be distributed, whether that's evenly among your children, with specific items going to specific people, or through whatever structure your Distribution Intent statement described.

Those three functions are real, they matter, and a properly drafted will accomplishes all of them well. But now for the part that gets skipped in most conversations about estate planning, and the part that causes the most expensive surprises: here is plainly what a will cannot do, no matter how carefully it's written or how recently it was signed.

A will cannot override a beneficiary designation. This is worth restating in the starkest terms possible, because it's the single most common source of the exact failure this book opened with. If your 401(k) beneficiary form names your first spouse, and your will leaves everything to your second spouse, the 401(k) still goes to the first spouse. The will has no authority over that account whatsoever. The same is true for life insurance, IRAs, and any account with payable-on-death or transfer-on-death instructions attached. These transfers happen by contract between you and the institution holding the account, and a will is simply not part of that contract. No language you add to a will, however explicit, changes where a beneficiary-designated asset goes.

A will cannot avoid probate. This surprises people who assume that having a will means their family skips the court process entirely. In fact, the opposite is closer to true — a will is a probate document. Its entire function depends on being filed with and validated by a probate court, and the assets it governs go through that process by definition. If avoiding probate delays and costs is a priority for you, a will alone doesn't accomplish that; the tools that actually achieve it, primarily a properly funded trust and non-probate titling, are covered in the next two chapters.

And a will cannot take effect while you're alive. This sounds obvious stated directly, but it's easy to lose sight of in practice. A will only activates after death, which means it provides zero protection during incapacity — if you have a stroke or develop dementia and are alive but unable to manage your affairs, your will does absolutely nothing to help your family act on your behalf. That gap is exactly what powers of attorney and healthcare directives exist to fill, and chapter five covers them in detail.

Understanding these limits isn't meant to diminish the will's importance. It's meant to correct a specific, common, and expensive misunderstanding: that having a will means your estate plan is complete. A will is one system out of four, doing its specific job over a specific portion of what you own. The rest of this chapter will help you write that will so it does its job as well as possible. But it will not, on its own, be the whole plan — and knowing that now, rather than discovering it the way Marilyn did, is the entire point of reading this book in order.

3.2 Reading a Will Clause by Clause

A will is built from a small number of standard clauses, and once you can recognize each one and understand what it's doing, you can read your own will — or a draft an attorney hands you — with real judgment instead of simply trusting that it must be fine because it looks official.

The specific bequests clause comes first in most wills, and it's the most straightforward: it names particular items or amounts going to particular people. Five thousand dollars to a niece, a specific piece of jewelry to a daughter, a collection of tools to a son. These are handled individually and separately from everything else, which is exactly why they matter — anything you want to go to a specific person rather than being divided proportionally needs to show up here, explicitly, rather than being left to chance within the larger estate.

After specific bequests comes the residuary clause, and this is where most of the actual value in most estates ends up passing, because it covers everything left over after specific bequests are satisfied and debts are paid. If your will says nothing more specific than "the residue of my estate to my children in equal shares," this single clause is doing almost all of the real work of distributing your wealth. A residuary clause with no clear instruction, or one that was never updated after a major life change, is one of the most common sources of confusion during probate, because it's often the largest bucket and the one people paid the least attention to when the will was drafted.

Within both specific bequests and the residuary clause, you'll often see a choice between two distribution methods that sound similar but produce very different outcomes: per stirpes and per capita. Per stirpes means that if one of your named beneficiaries dies before you, that beneficiary's share passes down to their own children, preserving the original branch of the family tree. Per capita means the share gets redistributed evenly among the surviving named beneficiaries instead, effectively skipping the deceased beneficiary's branch entirely. Picture three children as beneficiaries, one of whom dies before the parent, leaving two children of their own. Under per stirpes, that deceased child's share is split between their two children, so the family line still receives a full third overall. Under per capita, that share is instead divided between the two surviving siblings, and the grandchildren receive nothing directly. Neither approach is universally correct, but the difference is significant enough that leaving it unspecified, or not understanding which one your document defaults to, can produce a result that has nothing to do with what you intended.

A simultaneous death clause addresses an uncomfortable but practical scenario: what happens if you and a beneficiary, often a spouse, die in the same event with no clear way to determine who survived the other. Without a clause addressing this, the legal presumption varies by state and can create real complications, including assets bouncing between two estates and being taxed or delayed twice. A well-drafted will simply states an assumption to resolve the ambiguity, which sounds minor until you consider how often it actually becomes relevant in accidents involving couples.

A no-contest clause, sometimes called an in terrorem clause, is a deterrent provision stating that any beneficiary who challenges the will in court forfeits whatever they were set to inherit under it. These aren't enforceable in every state and aren't relevant to every family, but where a will makes noticeably unequal provisions among children, or disinherits someone entirely, this clause can meaningfully discourage a contest from a beneficiary who has something real to lose by trying.

And then there's the personal property memorandum, a separate, simpler document referenced by the will that lets you list who receives specific items of tangible personal property — furniture, art, family heirlooms, the dining table three siblings all independently remember as "always meant for them." Because this is a separate memorandum rather than part of the will itself, most states allow it to be updated without the formality of re-executing the entire will, which makes it one of the most useful tools available for preventing exactly the kind of dispute where the dollar value of an item is trivial but the emotional stakes are not.

Now put this to a practical test. Imagine a will that includes a residuary clause splitting the estate equally among three named children, a specific bequest of a car to the eldest, and a signature page with the testator's signature and one witness. Read that description again and see if you can identify what's missing before continuing. There are three deliberate gaps in it: no per stirpes or per capita language is specified, meaning what happens to a deceased child's share is left to the state's default rule rather than the testator's actual wishes; no personal property memorandum is referenced, leaving every non-cash item without specific instructions to be fought over inside the residuary split; and only one witness is listed, which fails the two-witness requirement most states impose, a gap covered directly in the next section. Spotting gaps like these in a document — your own or a draft in front of you — is the actual skill this section is trying to build, and it's a skill you now have.

3.3 Making the Signature Hold Up

A perfectly worded will that isn't executed correctly is not a will. It's a piece of paper, and probate courts do not treat good intentions as a substitute for proper execution. This section covers the mechanics of signing, because getting this part wrong is one of the most common and most entirely avoidable ways an otherwise sound plan collapses.

Most states require a will to be signed by the testator — the person making the will — in the presence of at least two witnesses, who must also sign the document themselves, typically in the testator's presence and in each other's presence as well. The witnesses don't need to know what the will says; they're attesting to the fact that they watched you sign it and that you appeared to be of sound mind and acting voluntarily, not to the contents of your decisions. It's standard practice, and generally wise, to choose witnesses who are not beneficiaries under the will, since some states restrict or complicate an interested witness's ability to also inherit under the same document they witnessed.

A self-proving affidavit is a separate notarized statement, typically signed at the same time as the will, in which the testator and witnesses swear under oath that the will was properly executed. Its purpose is almost entirely practical: without it, if the will is ever challenged, the witnesses may need to be tracked down and brought to testify in person, years or decades later, that they actually witnessed the signing. With a self-proving affidavit on file, the will can typically be admitted to probate without that step, which matters enormously if a witness has since moved away, become difficult to locate, or died. This single notarized page is one of the cheapest, simplest additions to a will and one of the most valuable if the will is ever questioned.

These requirements are not identical everywhere. Witness counts, notarization rules, and what qualifies as a valid execution vary by state, and a will validly executed in one state is generally honored in another, but the safest approach if you split time between states or plan to relocate is to have your will reviewed against the specific requirements of wherever you currently reside, rather than assuming a document drafted years ago in a different state still meets every local formality.

Handwritten wills, sometimes called holographic wills, are recognized in some states under specific conditions and rejected outright in others, and even where they're accepted, they fail more often in practice than formally executed wills, usually because they lack witnesses, use ambiguous language that a court has to interpret rather than simply follow, or fail to clearly revoke earlier wills, leaving conflicting documents behind. A handwritten will is better than nothing, but it should be treated as a stopgap, not a long-term plan.

DIY will software and online templates occupy a genuinely useful but limited role. For a simple estate — modest assets, no business interests, no unusual family structure, clear and uncontested distribution wishes — reputable software can produce a legally valid will, particularly if it walks you through your state's specific witnessing requirements rather than applying a generic template. Where DIY tools become risky is at exactly the points this book keeps returning to: blended families, disinheriting a child, a family business, significant unequal distributions, or any situation where the plain language on the page needs to anticipate a challenge. In those cases, the cost of an attorney is small relative to the cost of a will that doesn't hold up.

When your circumstances change and your will needs updating, you have two options, and the size of the change should decide which one you use. A codicil is a short, separately executed amendment to an existing will, appropriate for small, specific changes — updating an executor, adjusting a single bequest. A full restatement, essentially a new will that revokes all prior versions, is the better choice for significant changes, or when multiple codicils have accumulated to the point where reading the original will alongside its amendments becomes confusing even for the people meant to interpret it. When in doubt, a full restatement is cleaner and safer than a codicil, because it leaves no ambiguity about which version of any given clause is currently in effect.

Before you sign anything, walk through this in order: confirm your state's exact witness and notarization requirements, gather witnesses who are not beneficiaries under the will, sign in front of them and have them sign in front of you and each other, complete the self-proving affidavit with a notary present, and then decide where the original will physically live. That last step matters more than people expect. Store the original in a fireproof, secure location, and make sure your named executor knows exactly where it is and how to access it — a will nobody can find is functionally identical to a will that was never written at all.

Chapter 4 — Use a Trust to Skip Probate

Few tools in estate planning are as widely misunderstood, in both directions, as the revocable living trust. Some people are told it will save them thousands in taxes and protect their assets from lawsuits. Others are told it's an unnecessary expense sold by attorneys padding their fees. Neither version is accurate, and the confusion costs people real money either way — either they pay for a trust expecting benefits it was never going to deliver, or they skip one that would have solved a genuine problem for their family. This section explains exactly what a trust does mechanically, what it actually accomplishes, and what it flatly does not, so you can make this decision based on your own situation rather than on whatever you last heard at a dinner party.

Start with the mechanics, because the terminology trips people up before the substance even enters the conversation. A revocable living trust involves three roles, and in the most common setup, one person fills all three simultaneously, which is part of why the structure confuses people at first. The grantor is the person who creates the trust and transfers assets into it — this is you. The trustee is the person who manages the trust's assets according to its written instructions — while you're alive and capable, this is also you, meaning you retain complete control over everything inside the trust exactly as if it were still titled in your own name. The beneficiary is whoever receives the benefit of the trust's assets, whether that's you during your lifetime or your heirs after your death. "Revocable" means precisely what it sounds like: you can change the trust's terms, add or remove assets, or dissolve it entirely at any point while you're alive and mentally competent, which is what distinguishes it sharply from the irrevocable trust varieties covered later in this chapter, where that flexibility is deliberately given up in exchange for other benefits.

Here is the part that actually matters, though, and the part most explanations skip past too quickly: creating a trust document changes nothing on its own. The trust only controls what's been legally retitled into its name — meaning your house deed reassigned to the trust, your bank and brokerage accounts retitled with the trust as owner, and so on. A signed trust document sitting in a drawer, holding nothing, protects nothing. This is worth flagging clearly here because the next chapter section deals with it directly, but it needs to be understood from the outset: the trust document is only step one of two, and the second step, funding it, is where the real work and the real value happen.

With the mechanics established, here's what a properly funded revocable living trust actually accomplishes, and there are three genuine benefits worth taking seriously.

The first and most significant is probate avoidance. Assets held inside a funded trust are not owned by you individually at the moment of your death — they're owned by the trust, which continues operating exactly as it did while you were alive, now under the direction of your named successor trustee, following instructions you wrote while you were still in control. Because the trust itself doesn't die, there's nothing for a probate court to process regarding those assets. They simply continue being administered by the trustee and distributed according to the trust's terms, typically in a fraction of the time and expense a probate proceeding would require, and without a court's ongoing supervision.

The second benefit is privacy. A will, once filed with a probate court, becomes a public record — anyone can request and read it, including exactly what you owned and who received what. A trust generally never gets filed with any court and never becomes public record in the same way, which means the details of what you owned and how you distributed it stay private, known only to the people directly involved. For families who'd rather not have their financial affairs available for public inspection, or who want to avoid the specific vulnerability of heirs being publicly identifiable as having just inherited money, this matters more than it might initially seem.

The third benefit is the one people underestimate the most, and it directly addresses the incapacity gap discussed in chapter three: seamless management if you become unable to handle your own affairs. Because you named a successor trustee when you created the trust, that person can step in immediately and manage the trust's assets on your behalf if you become incapacitated, without needing a court to appoint them as guardian or conservator first. There's no petition, no hearing, no court supervision going forward — just a pre-named, trusted person continuing to pay bills, manage investments, and handle property exactly as the trust instructs, precisely at the moment your family would otherwise be facing the expensive, slow guardianship process described in chapter one.

Now for the two myths that need killing outright, because they persist despite being simply untrue, and believing them leads people to expect protection they don't actually have.

The first myth is that a revocable living trust saves income tax. It does not. While the trust is revocable and you're alive, it's treated as a disregarded entity for tax purposes — every dollar of income the trust's assets generate is reported and taxed on your own personal tax return exactly as if the trust didn't exist. There is no income tax advantage whatsoever to this structure, and anyone suggesting otherwise is either confused or trying to sell you something you don't need.

The second myth is that a revocable living trust protects your assets from your own creditors or from lawsuits while you're alive. It does not, for a simple reason: because you retain complete control over the trust as both grantor and trustee, and can revoke it or pull assets back out at any time, the law treats those assets as fully yours for purposes of creditor claims and legal judgments against you personally. Genuine creditor protection requires giving up that control entirely, which is what irrevocable trusts do, at a real cost in flexibility, and which section 4.3 of this chapter will cover.

What a revocable living trust actually offers, then, is not tax savings and not creditor protection. It's a faster, more private transfer of assets to your heirs and a built-in safety net if you become incapacitated — genuine, valuable benefits, but specific ones. Whether those specific benefits are worth the cost and effort of setting one up, compared to relying on a well-drafted will alone, depends entirely on your own situation: the size and complexity of your estate, how much you value privacy, and how much weight you place on avoiding the guardianship process if incapacity strikes before death does. The next section walks through what actually funding a trust requires, and the case file that follows shows exactly what happens when that step gets skipped.

4.2 Funding: The Step Everyone Skips

If section 4.1 established anything, it's that a trust document alone protects nothing. The trust only governs what's actually been retitled into its name, and that retitling process — called funding — is where the real work of setting up a trust happens. It's also, reliably, the step people skip, because it's tedious, it involves paperwork with multiple institutions, and it doesn't feel like the important part compared to the meeting where you signed the trust itself. This section exists because that instinct is exactly backward.

Start with real estate, since it's usually the most valuable asset most people own and the one funding failures hurt the most. Retitling a house into a trust requires preparing and recording a new deed that transfers ownership from you personally to the trust, filed with the county recorder or land records office wherever the property sits. This isn't a document you sign once and forget — it needs to actually be recorded, and if you own property in more than one state, each property needs its own deed prepared and recorded according to that state's specific requirements, since a deed valid in one state doesn't automatically transfer property in another.

Bank and brokerage accounts require a different but equally concrete process: contacting each institution directly and either retitling the existing account into the trust's name or opening a new account in the trust's name and transferring the balance over. Every bank, every brokerage firm, every account you listed on your Estate Map back in chapter two needs this done individually — there's no single filing that handles all of them at once, which is exactly why this step gets abandoned partway through by people who start strong and lose momentum after the third or fourth phone call.

If you hold an interest in an LLC or other business entity, that interest can typically be assigned into the trust through a formal assignment document, though this needs to be done carefully and often in coordination with whatever the operating agreement itself allows or requires, since some agreements restrict how ownership interests can be transferred, even into your own trust. Chapter nine covers business succession in more depth, but the funding step here is simple to state even if the paperwork takes some care: don't assume an LLC interest is automatically covered by the trust just because you meant it to be.

Retirement accounts are the deliberate, important exception to all of this, and it's worth being explicit about why. You should generally not retitle a 401(k) or IRA into a trust's name. These accounts already pass by beneficiary designation, completely independent of the will and largely independent of the trust structure, and moving ownership into a trust can trigger unintended and sometimes severe tax consequences, since it may be treated as a full distribution of the account. Instead, retirement accounts stay titled in your own name, and you handle them through the beneficiary designation itself — naming individuals directly, or in some cases naming the trust as beneficiary, a more advanced strategy covered in chapter eight when the tax mechanics are relevant. The point here is simply that leaving retirement accounts out of the trust isn't an oversight. It's correct.

Now, the case that shows exactly what happens when this entire process gets skipped. A couple paid an attorney roughly twelve hundred dollars to draft a complete revocable living trust — a fair, reasonable price for solid legal work. They signed it, felt appropriately proud of having handled something most of their friends kept putting off, and filed the documents away. What they never did was the follow-up work: no deed was ever recorded transferring their house into the trust, no accounts were ever retitled, nothing was ever assigned. Everything they owned remained, on paper, exactly as it had been titled before the trust existed. When the husband died eight years later, his family discovered that the trust, despite being properly drafted and properly signed, owned nothing at all. Every asset had to go through probate anyway, on the same timeline and at roughly the same cost it would have taken without a trust in the picture, because the trust had never actually received anything to protect. The family paid for the trust and paid for probate. That is the single most expensive and most common way this entire structure fails, and it fails silently, because nothing about an unfunded trust looks wrong from the outside until someone dies and the paperwork is finally tested.

This is exactly why every trust should be paired with what's called a pour-over will — a short will whose only real function is to state that anything you own outside the trust at death should pour over into it, still passing to the same beneficiaries under the same terms, just by a slightly longer route through probate first. A pour-over will is a backstop, not a substitute. It catches whatever funding missed, whether that's an asset you forgot to retitle or something you acquired after the trust was created and never got around to adding. It does not eliminate the cost of skipping funding — the asset it catches still goes through probate to get there — but it prevents the far worse outcome of an asset falling entirely outside your plan with no instructions attached to it at all.

Use this as your working checklist, organized by category rather than as a one-time task: real estate, retitled by deed and recorded in every relevant county. Bank and brokerage accounts, retitled individually with each institution. Business interests, formally assigned according to the governing agreement. Retirement accounts, deliberately left outside the trust and handled instead through direct beneficiary designation. Go through your Estate Map from chapter two, asset by asset, and confirm — don't assume, confirm — that each one has actually been moved. A trust that exists on paper but hasn't been funded isn't a weaker version of protection. It's no protection at all, dressed up as something that looks like it.

4.3 The Irrevocable Trust Family, Briefly

Everything covered so far in this chapter concerns the revocable living trust, which you control completely and can dissolve at will. There's an entirely separate category worth knowing about, even if most readers of this book will never need it: irrevocable trusts, a family of specialized tools that trade away control in exchange for something you can't get any other way, usually tax reduction or asset protection.

The trade at the center of every irrevocable trust is the same, regardless of which variety you're looking at. Once assets go into an irrevocable trust, you generally can't take them back, can't change the terms unilaterally, and no longer directly control them — a separate trustee, who cannot be you in most structures designed for tax purposes, manages the assets according to terms you can no longer alter. In exchange for giving up that control and reversibility, these structures can accomplish things a revocable trust simply cannot: removing assets from your taxable estate, protecting assets from creditors because you no longer legally own them, or preserving eligibility for government benefits for a beneficiary who couldn't otherwise receive an inheritance directly.

An irrevocable life insurance trust, usually called an ILIT, owns a life insurance policy on your life instead of you owning it personally, which keeps the policy's death benefit out of your taxable estate — relevant primarily for estates large enough to face federal or state estate tax exposure, a threshold covered specifically in chapter seven.

A spousal lifetime access trust, or SLAT, lets one spouse transfer assets out of their estate into an irrevocable trust for the benefit of the other spouse, who can still indirectly access the funds through that spouse's access to the trust, while the assets themselves are removed from the transferring spouse's taxable estate. This is a strategy aimed specifically at couples with estates large enough to be actively managing exposure to the estate tax exemption threshold.

A qualified terminable interest property trust, known as a QTIP, provides income to a surviving spouse for their lifetime while ultimately directing the remaining principal to beneficiaries the first spouse chose — commonly children from a prior marriage. This is the primary tool chapter nine relies on for blended families, letting you provide for a second spouse without permanently disinheriting children from an earlier relationship.

A credit shelter trust, sometimes called a bypass trust, is an older strategy for married couples designed to use both spouses' individual estate tax exemptions rather than losing the first spouse's exemption entirely. Its usefulness has narrowed considerably since portability rules were introduced allowing a surviving spouse to inherit their deceased spouse's unused exemption directly, but it still has situational relevance depending on state estate tax rules, which chapter seven addresses.

A special needs trust holds assets for the benefit of a beneficiary with a disability without disqualifying them from means-tested government benefits like Medicaid or Supplemental Security Income, which would otherwise be lost if that beneficiary received an inheritance directly in their own name. Chapter nine covers this in detail, because getting it wrong can cost a vulnerable beneficiary access to benefits they depend on.

A spendthrift trust restricts a beneficiary's ability to access trust principal directly and shields the assets from that beneficiary's own creditors, relevant for a beneficiary with credit problems, poor financial judgment, or a high-conflict marriage where asset protection is a real concern.

And a charitable remainder trust provides income to you or another named beneficiary for a set period or lifetime, with whatever remains afterward going to a charity of your choosing, offering a current tax deduction and income stream in exchange for the eventual charitable gift.

Seven names, and the honest truth is that most readers of this book need to seriously discuss zero or one of them with an estate attorney, not all seven. The ILIT and SLAT become relevant primarily as your estate approaches or exceeds the exemption thresholds discussed in chapter seven. The QTIP becomes relevant specifically if you're in a second marriage with children from a prior relationship. The special needs trust becomes relevant only if you have a beneficiary receiving means-tested government benefits. The spendthrift trust becomes relevant if a specific beneficiary has a demonstrated pattern of financial instability or creditor exposure. The credit shelter trust and charitable remainder trust are more situational still, worth a passing question to an attorney but rarely the deciding factor for most families. Read back through your Estate Map and your Distribution Intent statement, see which of these triggers actually describes your circumstances, and bring only that specific question to a professional. Everything else on this list, for most people, can be read once, understood, and set aside without a second thought.

Chapter 5 — Protect Yourself While You're Still Here

Every chapter so far has quietly assumed a certain order of events: you plan, time passes, and eventually you die, at which point the will, the trust, and the beneficiary forms all activate and do their jobs. That assumption is worth challenging directly, because it's not how most people's timelines actually unfold, and the gap it creates is one of the most expensive and most avoidable failures in this entire book.

Incapacity — a stroke, a serious accident, the gradual onset of dementia, a medical event that leaves you alive but unable to manage your own affairs — is considerably more common than sudden, uncomplicated death, and for a meaningful share of people, it arrives well before death does, sometimes years before. This isn't a comfortable thing to plan around, which is exactly why so many people don't, but the sequence matters enormously to the plan you're building. A will, as chapter three made clear, does nothing while you're alive. A trust, even a fully funded one, only helps with incapacity if you specifically built that function into it and named a successor trustee ready to step in. Without a separate document specifically empowering someone to act on your behalf while you're alive but unable to, your family faces exactly the guardianship courtroom scenario described back in chapter one — a slow, public, expensive court process to get someone legally authorized to pay your mortgage, manage your investments, or even access your own bank accounts on your behalf.

The tool that closes this gap is the durable power of attorney for financial matters, and it deserves careful attention because the details inside it determine whether it actually works when your family needs it, or sits uselessly, technically valid but practically useless because a bank won't honor it.

Start with the word "durable," because it's doing real legal work in that phrase and isn't just decoration. A standard power of attorney, without the durability language, automatically terminates the moment you become incapacitated — which defeats the entire purpose, since incapacity is precisely the scenario you're trying to plan for. A durable power of attorney is specifically drafted to remain in effect through incapacity, continuing to authorize your named agent to act on your behalf exactly when that authority matters most. Any power of attorney you create as part of this planning process needs this durability language included explicitly; without it, you've created a document that works perfectly for every situation except the one you actually needed it for.

From there, you face a choice between two structures: immediate and springing. An immediate power of attorney takes effect the moment you sign it, giving your named agent authority to act on your behalf right away, even while you're fully capable of handling your own affairs yourself. A springing power of attorney, by contrast, only takes effect once a specific triggering condition is met, typically a determination by one or two physicians that you've become incapacitated. The appeal of springing authority is understandable — it feels safer to know the document can't be used until it's actually needed, rather than handing someone legal authority over your finances today. But springing powers carry a real practical cost: activating them requires the very process you were trying to avoid, since a bank or financial institution will often want to see the physician certifications before honoring the agent's authority, adding delay and friction at exactly the moment your family needs speed. Many estate planning professionals lean toward immediate powers of attorney specifically because they avoid this activation bottleneck, paired with the understanding that the document simply sits unused until it's needed, since your named agent has no obligation to act on your behalf before you actually want them to.

The scope of authority you grant matters just as much as when it activates. A durable power of attorney can be drafted broadly, giving your agent authority over essentially all of your financial affairs — banking, investments, real estate transactions, tax filings, insurance — or it can be limited to specific, named powers only. For the purpose this chapter is addressing, closing the incapacity gap completely, broad authority is generally what you want, since a narrowly drafted power of attorney that happens to omit exactly the authority your family needs in the moment provides little practical advantage over having nothing at all.

One power worth naming specifically, because it's often left out by default and matters more than people expect, is gifting authority. Without explicit language authorizing your agent to make gifts on your behalf, an agent generally cannot give away your assets, even for purposes that seem obviously reasonable, like continuing an established pattern of family gifting for tax planning purposes, or paying for a grandchild's education the way you always have. If ongoing gifting has been part of your financial life, or might become part of a tax strategy discussed in chapter seven, explicit gifting authority needs to be written into the document itself rather than assumed.

Finally, and this is a detail that trips up more families than almost anything else in this chapter: banks and financial institutions vary considerably in what they'll actually accept, and a power of attorney that's entirely valid under state law can still be rejected or delayed by an individual institution's internal compliance policies, particularly if the document is more than a few years old or wasn't drafted using language the institution's legal department recognizes. Some banks require their own specific power of attorney form to be signed in addition to, or instead of, a general one from an attorney. The only way to close this gap completely is proactively: after your power of attorney is signed, contact each major financial institution where you hold accounts, ask whether they have specific requirements or their own preferred form, and if so, complete it now, while you're able to, rather than leaving your agent to discover the obstacle later, at the exact moment they're trying to use the authority you gave them.

Done properly — durable, with a clear immediate-versus-springing decision made deliberately rather than by default, broad in scope, explicit about gifting, and confirmed with your actual banks — a financial power of attorney accomplishes quietly and cheaply what a guardianship proceeding accomplishes slowly and expensively: someone you trust, acting on your behalf, the moment you need them to.

5.2 The Healthcare Documents Nobody Wants to Think About

Financial power of attorney handles money. It does nothing for the decisions that matter most during a medical crisis — who talks to your doctors, who decides whether to continue or stop a treatment, who has legal access to your medical records at all. That's a separate set of documents, and it deserves the same careful attention as the financial side, because vague healthcare wishes fail people just as often as missing financial authority does, just in a more painful way.

The advance directive, sometimes called a living will depending on the state, is where you put your actual medical wishes in writing — the kinds of treatment you would or wouldn't want under specific circumstances, particularly around end-of-life care. It works alongside, not instead of, a healthcare proxy, which names the specific person legally authorized to make medical decisions on your behalf when you're unable to make them yourself. Some states combine both functions into a single document; others keep them separate. Either way, you need both pieces covered: written guidance about your wishes, and a named person empowered to act on that guidance and make the judgment calls the written document can't fully anticipate.

A HIPAA authorization is a smaller document that solves a specific, frustrating problem: federal privacy law restricts who can access your medical information, and without explicit written authorization, even your spouse or adult child may be legally blocked from getting a straight answer from a hospital about your condition, regardless of how urgently they need one. This is often the document families discover they're missing at the worst possible moment, standing in a hospital hallway being told that privacy rules prevent a doctor from speaking with them. A signed HIPAA authorization, naming specific people who can receive your medical information, removes that obstacle entirely and should be treated as a companion document to your healthcare proxy rather than an afterthought.

Where applicable, a POLST or MOLST — Physician Orders for Life-Sustaining Treatment or Medical Orders for Life-Sustaining Treatment, depending on the state — is a different kind of document entirely from the advance directive. It's a medical order, signed by a physician after a direct conversation with you, translating your wishes into specific, actionable instructions that emergency responders and hospital staff follow immediately, without needing to interpret a broader document first. These are generally intended for people with serious or advanced illness, not as a universal document everyone needs, and they're created in consultation with a doctor rather than filled out independently, but where they apply, they carry a level of immediate, on-the-ground authority that a standard advance directive doesn't.

One category most standard templates leave out entirely, and one worth addressing directly given how common cognitive decline has become, is dementia-specific guidance. A typical advance directive is built around acute medical crises — a specific injury or sudden illness — and says very little about the slow, gradual decline that dementia often involves, where there's no single crisis moment but rather a long period of diminishing capacity. Useful dementia-specific instructions address questions a standard directive doesn't: at what point, if any, would you want life-sustaining treatment withheld for an unrelated condition given an advanced dementia diagnosis; what are your wishes regarding artificial nutrition and hydration specifically in the context of a progressive, irreversible cognitive decline rather than a sudden medical event; and who has authority to make placement decisions about long-term care if you're unable to communicate that yourself. These aren't questions most people enjoy sitting with, but leaving them unaddressed means your healthcare agent is left guessing during exactly the kind of prolonged, ambiguous decline where guessing wrong causes the most family conflict.

This brings up the core problem with how most people approach these documents in the first place: vague language. "No heroic measures" is the phrase that shows up constantly in advance directives, and it sounds clear until someone actually has to apply it. What counts as heroic. Is a ventilator heroic if it's temporary and recovery is likely, but not heroic if recovery is unlikely. Is a feeding tube heroic. The phrase provides no actual guidance to the person standing in the hospital room trying to honor your wishes, and it often paralyzes an agent precisely because they don't want to guess wrong about something this consequential, leading to decisions being deferred, prolonged, or handed to whichever family member argues most forcefully in the moment.

Usable guidance replaces vague phrases with specific scenarios and specific answers. Rather than "no heroic measures," a more useful instruction addresses conditions directly: if I am in a persistent vegetative state with no reasonable expectation of recovery, I do not want to be kept alive by artificial means. If I have a terminal illness and treatment would only prolong the dying process without meaningful benefit, I want comfort care rather than aggressive intervention. If there is a reasonable chance of meaningful recovery, I want treatment continued. This level of specificity gives your healthcare agent something to actually apply, rather than a phrase they have to interpret under pressure, often while other family members are watching and disagreeing.

Getting to this level of clarity requires an actual conversation, not just a form filled out alone at a kitchen table. Sit down with whoever you're naming as your healthcare agent and walk through a short set of direct questions together: what does a meaningful quality of life look like to you, specifically. Under what circumstances would you want treatment stopped rather than continued. How do you feel about artificial nutrition and hydration if there's no reasonable prospect of recovery. Is there a difference in your mind between a temporary intervention meant to get you through a crisis and an intervention meant to sustain a permanent, unchanging condition. Who else in the family needs to hear these answers directly from you, in your own words, so they're not hearing them secondhand from your agent during a moment of crisis. This conversation, more than any document, is what actually protects your agent from having to guess — and protects your family from the kind of conflict that erupts when people are forced to interpret silence instead of acting on something you actually said.

5.3 Long-Term Care: The Biggest Threat to Everything Else

Of everything covered in this book, long-term care costs pose the single largest financial threat to an estate, larger in most cases than estate taxes, larger than probate fees, larger than nearly anything else discussed so far — and it's frequently the piece left out of estate planning conversations entirely, because it feels more like a health topic than a legal one. It belongs squarely in this book, because an estate plan that ignores it can be technically flawless in every other respect and still be wiped out by a single extended nursing home stay.

Costs for extended care — whether in-home care, assisted living, or a skilled nursing facility — vary enormously by region and level of care needed, and any specific figure quoted today will be outdated within a few years given how consistently these costs have risen. What matters more than a specific number is the general shape of the problem: extended nursing home care commonly runs into six figures annually in many parts of the country, and even a few years of care at that level can consume savings that took a lifetime to build, regardless of how carefully everything else in an estate plan was structured. Anyone doing serious planning should look up current costs specific to their region rather than relying on a national average, since the range between a rural area and a major metropolitan region can be dramatic.

Medicaid, the government program that covers long-term care costs for people who qualify, becomes relevant to many families precisely because private savings run out. But qualifying for Medicaid isn't as simple as having low income at the moment care is needed — it involves a look-back period, typically five years, during which the program examines whether assets were given away or transferred for less than fair value in an apparent attempt to artificially reduce assets to qualify. Transfers made within that window can trigger a penalty period, delaying

Medicaid eligibility for a length of time tied to the value transferred. This is why last-minute asset transfers made in a panic once a diagnosis arrives are far less effective, and often far more complicated, than planning done years in advance, before any need is on the horizon.

Long-term care insurance exists specifically to address this risk, and it comes in two broad forms worth understanding as distinct products rather than variations on the same thing. Traditional long-term care insurance functions like standard insurance: you pay premiums, and if you need qualifying care, the policy pays out toward those costs, typically up to a daily or monthly benefit limit and a maximum benefit period. Its drawback is the one that discourages many people from buying it: if you die without ever needing long-term care, the premiums paid over the years are simply gone, providing no benefit at all. Hybrid long-term care policies, often combined with life insurance or an annuity, address that specific concern directly — if you never need long-term care, the policy still pays a death benefit to your heirs, meaning the premiums aren't lost regardless of how things unfold. Hybrid policies typically cost more upfront and may offer a lower long-term care benefit than a comparable traditional policy, but for people uncomfortable with the idea of paying into coverage they might never use, the guaranteed payout removes that specific hesitation.

An asset protection trust — an irrevocable trust specifically structured to hold assets outside your countable estate for Medicaid eligibility purposes — exists as a more aggressive tool for this specific risk, but it comes with real limitations that keep it from being a fit for most people. Because it's irrevocable, you give up direct control over the assets placed inside it, the same fundamental trade-off discussed with every irrevocable trust in chapter four. And because Medicaid's five-year look-back applies to transfers into this kind of trust exactly as it applies to any other transfer, the trust only provides protection if it's established at least five years before care is actually needed — meaning it's a tool for people planning well ahead of any anticipated need, not a solution available once a diagnosis has already arrived. It tends to make sense in fairly narrow circumstances: generally for people with meaningful but not extremely large assets, who want realistic protection against a long-term care event wiping out an inheritance they intend to leave, and who are comfortable planning many years in advance and giving up direct access to the assets involved.

To translate all of this into an actual decision, work through it based on your age and asset level rather than trying to hold every option in mind at once. If you're in your fifties or early sixties and your assets fall in the low-to-middle range this book's audience typically occupies, traditional or hybrid long-term care insurance, purchased while you're still healthy enough to qualify at reasonable rates, is usually the most practical and directly effective option, since premiums rise steeply with age and health complications can eliminate eligibility entirely. If you're already in your late sixties or beyond and haven't purchased coverage, hybrid policies are often more accessible than traditional ones at this stage, though premiums will be higher than they would have been a decade earlier. If your assets are substantial enough that self-funding a few years of care wouldn't meaningfully threaten your family's financial security, formal long-term care insurance becomes less essential, though the guardianship and incapacity protections covered earlier in this chapter still matter regardless of asset level. And if you're specifically focused on Medicaid planning and asset protection rather than insurance, and you're comfortable committing to an irrevocable structure at least five years before you expect to need care, an asset protection trust deserves a direct conversation with an elder law attorney — a narrow but real fit for a specific type of planner. Whichever path applies to you, the point of this section is the same one that's run through this entire chapter: the biggest threats to your estate often arrive while you're still alive, and the planning that protects against them can't wait until the will and trust are finished and filed away.

Chapter 6 — Control the Assets Wills Can't Touch

Every previous chapter has circled back to the same warning without fully unpacking it: beneficiary designations override the will, completely and automatically, for the assets they cover. This chapter is where that warning finally gets the full treatment it deserves, because it's arguably the single most important chapter in this book for the average reader. Not because trusts aren't valuable, not because wills don't matter, but because the failure mode this chapter addresses is the most common, the most quietly dangerous, and the easiest to fix once you actually see it clearly.

Start with the scenario that opened this book, because it's worth returning to now with full context. Tom updated his will after marrying Marilyn. He never went back and updated the beneficiary form on his 401(k), which still listed his first wife from a marriage that had ended nearly two decades earlier. This is not a rare or unusual failure — it's one of the most common patterns in estate settlement, precisely because updating a will feels like the comprehensive fix, the one document that surely covers everything. It doesn't. The beneficiary form is a separate, standalone contract between the account holder and the financial institution, and it operates entirely independent of whatever the will says, no matter how recently the will was signed or how explicitly it states an intention to override prior arrangements. Courts have ruled on this pattern repeatedly and consistently: the beneficiary form controls, full stop, regardless of what a later will attempts to say. An ex-spouse named decades earlier and never removed will inherit exactly as if the divorce, the remarriage, and the new will never happened.

A second common failure sits quietly on the same forms and causes just as much damage, though it's less dramatic than an ex-spouse inheriting: the contingent beneficiary line left blank. Most beneficiary forms ask for two things — a primary beneficiary, who receives the asset under normal circumstances, and a contingent beneficiary, who receives it only if the primary beneficiary has already died. People reliably fill in the primary line and skip the contingent one, either because it feels redundant at the time or because the form simply wasn't explained clearly when it was completed. The problem surfaces only in a specific, unlucky sequence: if the named primary beneficiary predeceases the account holder and no contingent beneficiary was ever named, the asset typically defaults back into the account holder's probate estate, pulling exactly the outcome — court involvement, delay, cost — that a well-designed beneficiary structure was supposed to avoid in the first place. A blank line that looked unimportant on a form filled out fifteen years ago becomes the reason an account ends up in probate after all.

A third failure hides in plain sight, on the second page of forms most people never fully read: per stirpes elections. Many beneficiary forms include an option, often presented as a simple checkbox, allowing the account holder to specify that if a named beneficiary predeceases them, that beneficiary's share passes down to their own children rather than being redistributed among the other named beneficiaries — the exact same per stirpes concept covered in chapter three's discussion of wills, but now living on a financial institution's form instead of in an attorney-drafted document. Because this option is usually buried past the primary fields most people focus on, it's frequently left unselected by default, which means the institution's standard rule applies instead — often a per capita result nobody consciously chose. A grandparent who assumed a deceased child's share would naturally flow to that child's own children may be surprised to learn, only when it matters, that the account's default rule redirected that share to the surviving siblings instead.

The fourth and most consequential trap on this list involves naming a minor child directly as a beneficiary on any account — a retirement account, a life insurance policy, anything with a beneficiary designation. Financial institutions cannot legally pay out a large sum directly to a minor. If a minor is named and the funds become payable while that child is still under eighteen, the result is not a simple, direct transfer — it typically requires a court-appointed conservator to manage the funds until the child reaches legal age, adding exactly the court supervision, cost, and delay this entire section of the book has been working to help you avoid. Worse, in many states, funds held this way are released to the child in a single lump sum the moment they turn eighteen, with no staggered distribution, no conditions, no consideration of whether an eighteen-year-old is actually prepared to manage a significant inheritance responsibly. The fix, generally, is never to name a minor directly. Instead, name a trust — either the revocable living trust from chapter four, if one exists and is structured to receive the funds, or a simpler standalone trust created specifically for this purpose — as the beneficiary, with instructions about timing and conditions that reflect the actual intentions in your Distribution Intent statement from chapter two.

Having seen all four traps clearly, the fix isn't complicated, but it requires actually doing something rather than assuming everything is fine because you remember filling the forms out correctly at some point. For every single account with a beneficiary designation — every retirement account from every employer you've ever had, every life insurance policy including small employer-provided ones, every payable-on-death or transfer-on-death account — contact the institution directly and request written confirmation of exactly who is currently listed as primary and contingent beneficiary. Don't rely on an old paper copy from your own files or on memory of what you filled in originally; request current confirmation directly from the custodian, since forms get updated, accounts get transferred between institutions during mergers, and old paperwork doesn't always survive the transition intact. Once you have that confirmation in hand for each account, compare it against your Distribution Intent statement and correct anything that doesn't match, including adding contingent beneficiaries wherever they're missing and replacing any minor's name with a trust. This process takes real time, account by account, but it's the single highest-leverage action in this entire book relative to the effort involved, because it directly closes the gap that caused the exact failure this book opened with.

6.2 Titling: The Other Way Assets Skip the Will

Beneficiary designations aren't the only mechanism that operates outside your will's control. How an asset is titled — the legal ownership structure attached to it — matters just as much, and it deserves the same careful scrutiny this chapter has already applied to beneficiary forms, because a surprising number of people use joint titling as an informal substitute for real planning, without understanding exactly what that substitution costs them.

Joint tenancy with right of survivorship is the most common titling arrangement people fall into, often without deliberately choosing it. When two people own an asset — a house, a bank account — as joint tenants with right of survivorship, the surviving owner automatically becomes the sole owner the instant the other owner dies, with no probate involvement whatsoever and no reference to either owner's will. This happens by operation of the titling itself, immediately and automatically, which is precisely why so many people default to it: it feels simple, it avoids probate entirely for that asset, and it requires no additional legal documents to accomplish.

Tenancy by the entirety is a related but distinct structure, available only to married couples in states that recognize it, offering the same automatic survivorship feature as joint tenancy but with an added layer of protection: neither spouse can transfer or encumber the property without the other's consent, and in most cases, a creditor pursuing only one spouse individually cannot reach property held this way. Where it's available, it's generally a stronger structure for married couples than standard joint tenancy, though it only applies to spouses and doesn't extend to other family relationships.

Community property, recognized in a handful of states, works differently still. Rather than each spouse owning a specific, separately identifiable share, most assets acquired during the marriage are considered equally owned by both spouses as a single unit, regardless of whose income purchased them or whose name appears on the title. Some community property states also offer a specific variant, community property with right of survivorship, which layers the same automatic transfer-at-death feature found in joint tenancy on top of the community property structure. Because these rules vary meaningfully by state and interact directly with how assets are taxed at death, anyone living in or moving to a community property state should have their specific situation reviewed against that state's particular rules rather than assuming the general concept applies uniformly everywhere.

Transfer-on-death and payable-on-death designations, already mentioned briefly in chapter two, deserve fuller treatment here because they function as a titling tool in their own right, applicable to accounts and, in many states, directly to real estate through what's often called a transfer-on-death deed. These designations let you name a beneficiary who receives the asset immediately upon your death, entirely outside probate, while you retain full ownership and control during your lifetime — unlike joint tenancy, the named person has no ownership interest and no access to the asset while you're alive. For many single people, or for anyone who wants the probate-avoidance benefit of joint titling without actually adding another owner during their lifetime, a transfer-on-death or payable-on-death designation accomplishes the same end result with considerably less risk, for reasons the rest of this section makes concrete.

That risk centers on a specific, common decision that feels harmless and often isn't: adding an adult child directly to a deed as a joint owner, usually done with the entirely reasonable intention of helping that child avoid probate on the family home. This move carries two costs that rarely get explained clearly at the moment the decision is made, and both are worth walking through with actual numbers rather than in the abstract.

The first cost is an unintended gift. Adding your adult child as a joint owner on your deed isn't a neutral administrative change — legally, you've just given that child an ownership interest in the property, valued at whatever percentage share their new ownership represents. If your home is worth six hundred thousand dollars and you add one child as a fifty percent joint owner, you've made a gift of roughly three hundred thousand dollars, whether or not either of you thought of it in those terms. Gifts above the annual exclusion amount, covered in more detail in chapter seven, need to be reported to the IRS on a gift tax return, and while most people won't owe actual gift tax due to the lifetime exemption also discussed there, the reporting obligation and the erosion of that lifetime exemption are real consequences of what felt like a simple paperwork change.

The second cost is more subtle and, for many families, ultimately more expensive: a forfeited step-up in basis. When you inherit an asset through a will or a properly structured trust, its cost basis for tax purposes generally resets to its fair market value on the date of death — a benefit called the step-up in basis, covered fully in chapter seven, which can eliminate capital gains tax entirely on appreciation that happened during the original owner's lifetime. But when your child receives ownership through joint titling added while you're alive, rather than through inheritance at death, the portion they received as a lifetime gift typically keeps your original cost basis rather than receiving that step-up. Here's the arithmetic made concrete: say you bought your home decades ago for one hundred thousand dollars, and it's worth six hundred thousand dollars today. If your child inherits it properly through your will or trust after your death, their basis resets to six hundred thousand dollars, and if they sell it soon after for close to that value, there's little or no capital gains tax owed. But if you'd instead added them as a fifty percent joint owner years earlier and they later sell their inherited share, their basis on that gifted portion remains tied to your original purchase price rather than the date-of-death value, potentially creating a capital gains tax bill on decades of appreciation that a properly structured inheritance would have eliminated entirely.

Put together, these two costs mean that adding a child to a deed to save on probate can end up costing far more than probate ever would have, through gift tax reporting complications and a lost step-up in basis that a transfer-on-death deed or a properly funded trust would have preserved while accomplishing the exact same probate-avoidance goal. Joint titling isn't inherently wrong, and it remains the right tool in specific situations, particularly between spouses. But using it as an informal substitute for real estate planning, added to a deed in a single conversation with a title company rather than considered as part of a full Estate Map and Distribution Intent, is a pattern this chapter exists specifically to interrupt.

6.3 The One-Page Conflict Check

Every piece of this book has been building toward a single moment, and this is it: laying every document you own side by side and checking, item by item, whether they actually agree with each other. This is the alignment audit, and it's the direct, practical answer to the exact failure that opened this book — a will and a beneficiary form that quietly contradicted each other for nineteen years before anyone noticed.

Pull out four things: your Estate Map from chapter two, complete with its probate and non-probate markings; your current will; your trust documents, if you have one, along with confirmation of what's actually been funded into it; and the written confirmations you gathered in section 6.1 from every institution holding an account with a beneficiary designation. Build a simple table, one row per asset, with columns for what your will says about that asset, what your trust says if the asset is meant to be included in it, what the current beneficiary form or titling actually shows, and a final column simply marked match or conflict.

Work through this line by line, without skipping anything on the assumption that it's probably fine. For each probate asset governed by your will, confirm the will's residuary and specific bequest language actually reflects your current Distribution Intent statement rather than an earlier version of your wishes. For each asset meant to be held in your trust, confirm it's actually been funded — retitled and recorded — rather than simply assumed to be included because the trust exists. For each account with a beneficiary designation, confirm the written custodian confirmation matches what you intended, including both primary and contingent beneficiaries, and confirm no minor is named directly anywhere on the list.

Contradictions surface in a small number of predictable patterns, and recognizing the pattern usually points directly to the fix. An asset appearing in both the will's specific bequests and a trust's asset schedule, assigned to two different people, means one of those documents is outdated and needs to be corrected to match your actual current intent. A beneficiary form still naming a former spouse alongside a will that leaves everything to a current one is the exact Tom-and-Marilyn pattern from this book's introduction, and it needs to be corrected with the institution directly, not through the will. An asset meant for the trust that's still titled in your individual name is an unfunded trust problem exactly like the one described in chapter four's case file, and the fix is completing the retitling, not rewriting any document. A blank contingent beneficiary line paired with a primary beneficiary who's now older and could plausibly predecease you is a gap that needs filling before it becomes a real problem rather than a theoretical one.

Once you've identified every contradiction, resolve each one and write the date next to it. This last step matters more than it might seem, because an unresolved conflict discovered today and left unresolved is functionally identical to never having found it at all — the value of this audit comes entirely from actually fixing what it reveals, not from the discovery itself. Set a realistic date for each fix based on what it requires: a beneficiary form correction might take a single phone call and be resolved this week, while an unfunded asset that needs a new deed prepared and recorded might reasonably take a month.

This one-page conflict matrix, more than any single document covered in this book, is what actually prevents accidental disinheritance. Not because any individual document was wrong when it was created, but because documents drift out of sync with each other over years of life changes, and nothing forces them back into alignment unless someone deliberately checks. You've just done that. Keep this page with your other estate planning documents, and revisit it at the same intervals chapter ten will recommend for reviewing the plan as a whole — because the alignment you've just achieved is only as durable as your discipline in checking it again the next time something in your life changes.

Chapter 7 — Cut Your Estate Tax Bill Legally

If there's one subject that generates more anxiety than it deserves for most readers of this book, it's estate tax. People picture the IRS taking a large chunk of whatever they leave behind, and that fear, more than almost any other single factor, drives some genuinely unnecessary decisions — awkward last-minute gifting, unnecessarily complicated trust structures, sometimes outright avoidance of the planning process altogether because it feels overwhelming before it's even begun. This chapter exists to separate the tax that technically exists in the law from the tax that actually applies to you, because for the large majority of people reading this book, the honest answer is going to be a relief.

Start with the number that matters most: the federal unified estate and gift tax exemption. For 2026, that exemption stands at fifteen million dollars per individual. This is the amount a single person can pass to their heirs, combined across lifetime gifts and assets left at death, before any federal estate tax applies at all. For a married couple, using a mechanism called portability that this section explains in detail, that combined shelter effectively reaches thirty million dollars. This figure is set directly in the tax code rather than being an inflation estimate for this particular year, following legislation passed in 2025 that removed the expiration date that had previously been scheduled to cut the exemption roughly in half at the end of that year. Beginning in 2027, the exemption resumes its usual pattern of annual inflation adjustment, meaning it will continue rising in future years rather than remaining fixed at this exact figure. Above the exemption amount, the federal estate tax rate reaches a flat forty percent —

a genuinely significant rate, which is exactly why it's worth being clear about who actually needs to think about it.

Here's the arithmetic that matters for most households working through this book: fifteen million dollars is an extraordinarily high threshold, one that the overwhelming majority of American households, including the great majority of readers with the kind of assets this book was written for, will never come close to reaching. If your estate — everything you own combined, including your home, retirement accounts, life insurance not held in an irrevocable trust, investments, and any business interest — totals meaningfully less than that figure, federal estate tax simply doesn't apply to you, and no amount of clever planning changes that fact because there's no tax to avoid in the first place. This is worth sitting with directly, because a significant portion of the anxiety people bring to estate planning is anxiety about a tax that, for them, was never actually a live concern.

Understanding portability matters even for couples who feel confident their combined estate falls well under the threshold, because it's one of the few pieces of this chapter that requires an affirmative action rather than simply applying automatically. When a married person dies, any portion of their individual fifteen-million-dollar exemption that goes unused doesn't automatically transfer to the surviving spouse. It has to be elected, and that election happens through a specific form: Form 706, the federal estate tax return, filed by the deceased spouse's executor. Here's the detail that trips up more families than it should: filing this return and making the portability election is required even when the estate is nowhere near large enough to actually owe any tax. An executor who reasonably assumes there's no reason to file a return, because the estate clearly isn't large enough to owe anything, can inadvertently cause the surviving spouse to permanently lose access to that unused exemption. If that surviving spouse's own assets grow substantially in later years, perhaps through a business's appreciation, an inheritance of their own, or simply a strong investment period, and their combined estate later approaches or exceeds their own individual exemption, they may find themselves without the extra shelter their spouse's unused exemption would have provided, solely because a form that seemed unnecessary at the time was never filed. For couples whose combined assets are comfortably below the threshold with no realistic path to growing near it, this may genuinely not matter. For couples with any meaningful uncertainty about future growth, a business interest, or significant life insurance, filing Form 706 to preserve portability, even when no tax is owed, is a low-cost, high-value action worth discussing with whoever handles the estate's tax filings.

For the reader working through this chapter and doing the honest math on their own situation, the most useful thing this section can offer is permission to feel the relief that's usually appropriate here. Take your Estate Map from chapter two, add up the fair market value of everything on it, including any life insurance death benefit not already held in an irrevocable trust, and compare that total honestly against the fifteen-million-dollar threshold, or thirty million if you're married and portability has been or will be properly elected. For the vast majority of people reading this book, this is the point where a substantial category of worry can be set aside entirely. Federal estate tax was never designed to reach ordinary households with a home, some retirement savings, and a comfortable but unremarkable net worth — it was designed, deliberately, to apply only to a genuinely small fraction of estates at the very top of the wealth distribution, and the 2025 legislative changes widened that gap further rather than narrowing it.

That relief, though, comes with an important redirection rather than a reason to close this chapter and move on. Federal estate tax may not apply to you. State-level estate and inheritance taxes are a different matter entirely, with thresholds in some states set dramatically lower than the federal figure, low enough that estates well within this book's target audience can find themselves owing real state tax even while owing nothing at all to the federal government. That's the subject the next section turns to directly, and for many readers, it will matter considerably more than anything covered so far in this chapter.

7.2 The Tax That Actually Reaches You

Here is the redirection this chapter has been building toward: federal estate tax, as the previous section established, simply doesn't apply to the overwhelming majority of people reading this book. But that relief can be misleading if it's the only thing you take away from this chapter, because a separate and considerably more reachable tax exists at the state level, and its thresholds sit nowhere near the generous federal exemption.

Twelve states and the District of Columbia currently impose their own estate tax, entirely separate from and in addition to the federal system, and several of these operate at exemption levels low enough to catch households that would never come close to owing anything federally. Massachusetts sets its exemption at two million dollars. Oregon sets its even lower, at one million dollars, a threshold that hasn't moved with inflation in years and consequently reaches further into ordinary estates every year that home values and retirement savings continue to grow. For a retired professional in the Boston or Portland area, a paid-off home combined with a lifetime of retirement savings and modest investments can cross either of these thresholds without the household ever feeling particularly wealthy — this is precisely the audience this book was written for, and precisely why this section, not the federal exemption discussion, is where many readers should actually be paying close attention.

A separate category of state tax works on an entirely different mechanism and deserves to be understood as distinct rather than folded into the estate tax conversation. An inheritance tax, unlike an estate tax, isn't based on the total size of the estate at all — it's calculated on what each individual beneficiary receives, at a rate that depends specifically on that beneficiary's relationship to the person who died. Five states currently impose this kind of tax. Nebraska is a particularly relevant example for the purposes of this book, because unlike many inheritance tax structures that exempt or heavily favor direct descendants, Nebraska applies its inheritance tax to adult children once their individual inheritance exceeds a fairly modest threshold, a detail that surprises people who assume, reasonably enough, that leaving money directly to their own children is the one scenario immune from this kind of tax. Other states in this category vary considerably in how they treat different relationships — a spouse is generally exempt everywhere, children often receive more favorable treatment than more distant relatives, but the specific rates and exemption amounts differ enough from state to state that a beneficiary's relationship to you, not just the total value of what they're receiving, becomes a genuinely relevant planning question.

Two structural details make this section worth more than a quick glance at your own state's rules. The first is domicile, the legal concept that determines which state actually has authority to tax your estate. Domicile isn't simply about where you happen to be living at the time of death — it's a more specific legal determination based on factors like where you're registered to vote, where your driver's license is issued, where you file resident income tax returns, and where you genuinely intend to make your permanent home. This matters directly for anyone who splits time between states, particularly retirees who spend part of the year in a lower-tax or no-tax state and part of the year somewhere with a state estate tax, without ever having formally and deliberately established domicile in the more favorable location. Simply owning a second home in Florida doesn't make Florida your domicile if every other indicator — your voter registration, your primary bank, where you actually spend most of your time — still points to Massachusetts. Establishing domicile deliberately, with the paperwork and consistent behavior to support it, is a meaningfully different thing than assuming it happens automatically because you'd prefer it to.

The second structural detail, and one that catches people who feel confident their home state has no estate tax at all, involves property owned in a second state. If you live in a state with no estate tax but own a vacation home, a piece of land, or any other real property physically located in a state that does impose one — Oregon or Massachusetts, for instance — that specific property can be pulled into that state's estate tax system based purely on its location, regardless of where you're domiciled and regardless of what your home state's own tax rules say. This is the same mechanism, familiar from chapter two, that triggers a second probate proceeding for out-of-state property, and it applies to state estate tax exposure in exactly the same way: the property's location, not your residence, determines which state's tax rules reach it.

Given all of this, the practical exercise this section asks of you is straightforward to describe even if it takes some genuine research to complete. Identify your own state of domicile and check whether it currently imposes an estate or inheritance tax, and at what threshold. Then do the same for every other state where you own real property, since each one may independently reach a piece of your estate regardless of what your home state does. This is a check worth running against current information rather than assumption, since these thresholds and the list of states imposing these taxes do shift over time as state legislatures revisit their own tax codes — what applies this year may not be exactly what applied five years ago, or what will apply five years from now.

7.3 What to Actually Do About It

Having separated the federal tax that rarely applies from the state-level taxes that reach much further, this final section turns to the practical strategies available to reduce exposure to whichever of these actually touches your situation. These strategies exist on a genuine ladder, arranged by how much net worth someone needs before a given rung becomes worth the effort, and one of the more useful things this section can do is help you identify honestly which rung you're standing on, so you can stop worrying about the strategies several rungs above you.

At the base of the ladder sits the annual gift tax exclusion, currently set at nineteen thousand dollars per recipient per year, and available to every taxpayer regardless of overall net worth. This allows you to give up to that amount to as many different individuals as you'd like each year, with no gift tax consequence and no reduction to your lifetime exemption at all — a married couple can combine their individual exclusions to give up to double that amount to a single recipient, such as an adult child, without any reporting requirement. For most readers of this book, particularly those confident they'll never approach either the federal or their state's estate tax threshold, this base rung is simply a convenient way to help family members during your lifetime rather than a tax strategy in any urgent sense — useful, but not something to feel pressure around unless it fits your broader financial picture.

One step up sits a lesser-known but genuinely valuable provision: direct payments for tuition or medical expenses, made straight to the educational institution or medical provider rather than to the individual benefiting from the payment, don't count against the annual exclusion or your lifetime exemption at all, regardless of the amount. Paying a grandchild's full college tuition directly to the university, no matter how large the sum, has no gift tax consequence whatsoever, provided the payment goes straight to the institution rather than passing through the student's own hands first. This is a meaningfully underused strategy for grandparents specifically, since it allows substantial support for education or healthcare with none of the exclusion limits that apply to ordinary cash gifts.

Slightly further up, 529 college savings plan superfunding allows a strategy specific to education planning: rather than contributing the standard annual exclusion amount each year, the IRS allows you to front-load five years' worth of annual exclusions into a single contribution to a 529 plan, treated for gift tax purposes as if it were spread evenly across those five years. This lets a grandparent or parent move a substantial lump sum into tax-advantaged educational savings in one transaction rather than waiting years to contribute incrementally, a genuinely useful tool for anyone with the resources to fund a grandchild's education meaningfully in one step.

The rungs above this point — GRATs, SLATs, ILITs, and charitable vehicles like the charitable remainder trust covered in chapter four — belong to a different category of net worth entirely, generally relevant only to households whose estates genuinely approach or exceed the federal exemption threshold, or in some cases a state threshold significant enough to justify the complexity and legal cost these structures involve. If your Estate Map from chapter two puts you meaningfully below fifteen million dollars individually, or thirty million as a couple with portability properly elected, and your state doesn't impose its own estate tax at a lower threshold you're approaching, these top-rung strategies are worth understanding conceptually, as this chapter and chapter four have provided, but not worth pursuing actively. They exist to solve a problem that, for the great majority of this book's readers, doesn't exist.

Before closing this chapter, it's worth making one final, somewhat counterintuitive point directly, because it runs against the instinct many people bring to this subject. For most readers whose estates fall below the relevant thresholds, gifting appreciated assets during your lifetime is often the wrong move, not the right one — and the reason comes back to the step-up in basis discussed in chapter six. An asset you continue to hold until death generally passes to your heirs with its cost basis reset to fair market value on your date of death, eliminating capital gains tax on decades of appreciation entirely. The same asset given away during your lifetime carries your original, lower cost basis forward to the recipient, meaning they inherit your capital gains tax exposure along with the asset itself. For someone who isn't approaching an estate tax threshold at all, there's no tax benefit to lifetime gifting sufficient to offset this cost — you'd be giving up a valuable tax benefit for your heirs in exchange for avoiding a tax you were never going to owe in the first place. The strategies at the top of this ladder exist specifically because, above a certain threshold, the estate tax savings outweigh the lost step-up. Below that threshold, for most people reading this book, holding rather than gifting is simply the better arithmetic, and knowing that is worth more than any of the advanced structures this section has described.

Chapter 8 — Pass Retirement Accounts Without Tax Shock

Every asset covered so far in this book has followed a version of the same underlying pattern: title it correctly, name the right beneficiary, align the paperwork, and it passes to your heirs efficiently. Retirement accounts break that pattern in a way that surprises even people who've done everything else in this book correctly, and it's worth understanding exactly why before walking through the mechanics, because the surprise here isn't about probate or contradictory paperwork. It's about a tax bill that was always there, quietly deferred, waiting for someone to eventually pay it.

Start with the concept that makes retirement accounts fundamentally different from almost everything else in your estate: income in respect of a decedent, a piece of tax terminology worth understanding even though it rarely comes up in ordinary conversation. Most income gets taxed when it's earned or received. A traditional 401(k) or IRA works differently by design — contributions went in before tax, the account grew tax-deferred for years or decades, and the tax bill on all of it was always meant to be paid eventually, just not yet. When the original owner dies before that deferred tax has been paid, the obligation doesn't disappear. It transfers directly to whoever inherits the account, who now owes ordinary income tax on withdrawals from an account they didn't personally earn the money in, simply because they're the one now required to eventually take it out. This is fundamentally different from inheriting a paid-off house or a brokerage account holding stock, where the tax question is about capital gains on appreciation, not about a full deferred income tax bill on the entire underlying value.

That distinction connects directly to the second reason retirement accounts behave differently from everything else covered in this book: they receive no step-up in basis. Chapter six and chapter seven both explained the step-up in basis as one of the most valuable, quietly powerful features of inheriting most other kinds of property — a stock portfolio or a home that appreciated significantly during your lifetime passes to your heirs with its cost basis reset to current fair market value, often eliminating capital gains tax on decades of growth in a single stroke. Retirement accounts don't work this way, because the money inside them was never taxed as capital gains to begin with — it's ordinary income that was simply deferred, not appreciated capital that qualifies for basis adjustment. An heir inheriting a traditional IRA worth four hundred thousand dollars isn't inheriting an asset with a stepped-up basis of four hundred thousand dollars that can be sold tax-free. They're inheriting an obligation to eventually withdraw that entire four hundred thousand dollars and pay ordinary income tax on it, at whatever their own tax bracket happens to be when the withdrawals occur.

The third reason retirement accounts sit apart from the rest of this book connects directly back to chapter six's central warning, though with even higher stakes than the beneficiary form issues covered there. A retirement account's beneficiary designation controls its distribution absolutely and completely, with no exception and no override available through a will or trust unless the account was specifically and correctly structured to name a trust as beneficiary, a more advanced arrangement covered later in this chapter. Everything chapter six said about beneficiary forms overriding wills applies here with particular force, because retirement accounts are frequently among the largest single assets a person owns, and the tax consequences of getting the beneficiary designation wrong compound the ordinary problems of a misdirected inheritance with the added complexity of exactly how that inheritance gets taxed once it lands with the wrong person or the wrong structure.

To see how dramatically these three factors change the outcome depending on who inherits the account, it's worth contrasting the two most common scenarios directly. When a surviving spouse inherits a retirement account from their deceased spouse, they generally have the option to complete what's called a spousal rollover — treating the inherited IRA as though it were their own account, rather than as an inherited account subject to the distribution rules that apply to other beneficiaries. This means the surviving spouse can continue contributing to it if they're still working, can delay withdrawals according to their own age rather than their deceased spouse's, and generally faces the most flexible and favorable set of rules available to any beneficiary of a retirement account. The deferred tax bill hasn't disappeared — it's still there, waiting in the account exactly as it was before — but the spouse gets to manage the timing of paying it largely on their own terms, much as the original owner would have.

An inherited IRA received by anyone other than a spouse works under an entirely different and considerably less forgiving set of rules, ones that changed substantially following legislation commonly referred to as the SECURE Act, which the next section covers in detail. For now, the essential point is this: a non-spouse beneficiary, typically an adult child, generally cannot treat the account as their own the way a surviving spouse can. They inherit it as a distinct account subject to mandatory distribution rules on a compressed timeline, meaning the deferred tax bill that took the original owner decades to build up now has to be substantially resolved within a much shorter window, often while that beneficiary is still working and already sitting in their own peak-earning tax bracket.

This is the surprise this chapter exists to prevent. A parent who spent decades responsibly contributing to a 401(k), watching it grow, and feeling genuinely good about the size of the balance they're leaving behind may not realize that the number on the account statement isn't the number their child actually receives. Layered underneath that balance sits a deferred tax bill that was always going to come due eventually — the only question estate planning can actually influence is who pays it, when, and how much of it can be managed strategically rather than absorbed all at once. The rest of this chapter walks through exactly what the current rules require, and what can be done, starting now, to keep that inherited tax bill from landing on your heirs any harder than it has to.

This confirms the outline's figures well — the 10-year rule, the eligible designated beneficiary categories, the RBD-triggered annual RMDs, and the age 73→75 shift are all accurate for 2026. Writing the paragraphs now.

8.2 The Rules That Changed Everything

Understanding why retirement accounts create tax exposure, as the previous section explained, only gets you halfway. The other half is understanding exactly how the current rules require that exposure to be resolved, because those rules changed dramatically under legislation commonly called the SECURE Act, and the version most people vaguely remember hearing about isn't quite the version actually in effect today.

Before this legislation, a non-spouse beneficiary who inherited a retirement account could generally stretch withdrawals across their own life expectancy, sometimes over several decades, keeping most of the account growing tax-deferred while taking relatively small required distributions each year. That option is gone for the great majority of people who inherit a retirement account today. In its place sits a considerably less forgiving structure: most non-spouse beneficiaries, most notably adult children inheriting from a parent, must now fully empty the inherited account by December 31 of the tenth year following the original owner's death. There's no flexibility to extend that deadline, and no benefit to waiting until the final year to withdraw everything at once, for reasons the next paragraph makes clear.

A narrow category of beneficiaries escapes this compressed timeline and retains something closer to the older, more favorable stretch treatment. These are called eligible designated beneficiaries, and the category is deliberately limited rather than broad. It includes a surviving spouse, who as covered in the previous section has separate and more favorable options entirely. It includes a minor child of the original account owner, though only until that child reaches the age of majority, at which point the ten-year clock begins running for them just as it would for any other beneficiary. It includes a beneficiary who is disabled or chronically ill under the specific definitions the tax code applies to those terms. And it includes any beneficiary who is not more than ten years younger than the original account owner, a category that occasionally captures a sibling or a much younger spouse who doesn't otherwise qualify under the marital exception. Outside of these specific categories, an adult child in ordinary circumstances, inheriting from a parent of typical age difference, falls into the standard ten-year rule with no exception available.

Here's the detail that catches even beneficiaries who know about the ten-year deadline and think they've planned around it. For years after this legislation first passed, considerable ambiguity existed about whether beneficiaries subject to the ten-year rule needed to take any distributions during that window at all, or whether they could simply wait and withdraw the entire balance at the very end. Final regulations resolved that ambiguity, and the resolution surprised many advisors who had been operating under the more flexible assumption. If the original account owner died on or after their required beginning date — the point at which they themselves would have been required to start taking their own required minimum distributions, currently age seventy-three and gradually rising toward seventy-five for younger account owners under a separate provision of the same legislative framework — then the beneficiary must take annual required minimum distributions during years one through nine of the ten-year window, not simply wait until year ten to empty the account in a single distribution. Missing one of these annual distributions can trigger a real IRS penalty, calculated as a percentage of the amount that should have been withdrawn. If the original owner died before reaching their required beginning date, the beneficiary has more flexibility about timing within the nine years, but the hard ten-year emptying deadline still applies regardless.

To make this concrete rather than abstract, walk through an example built around numbers many readers of this book will recognize as realistic for their own situation. A parent dies holding a traditional IRA worth six hundred thousand dollars, having already begun taking required minimum distributions themselves, meaning they died after their required beginning date. Their adult child, an ordinary designated beneficiary with no exception available, inherits the account and is now in their peak earning years, perhaps in their late forties or early fifties, sitting in a meaningfully higher marginal tax bracket than either of their parents occupied during retirement. That child must take annual distributions across nine years and fully empty the account by the end of year ten. If the six hundred thousand dollars is withdrawn in anything close to equal installments, that adds roughly sixty thousand dollars of ordinary taxable income annually for a decade — income stacked directly on top of that child's own salary, in their own already-elevated tax bracket, at their own marginal rate rather than the presumably lower rate their retired parent might have paid taking the same withdrawals gradually over their own remaining lifetime.

Depending on that child's specific bracket, a meaningful share of each year's inherited distribution can be lost to federal income tax alone before state tax is even considered, and the elevated income can carry secondary consequences worth anticipating — potentially pushing the beneficiary into a higher bracket for other income earned that same year, or affecting eligibility for certain tax credits and deductions that phase out at higher income levels. The six-hundred-thousand-dollar number on the account statement, in other words, was never really six hundred thousand dollars of after-tax inheritance. A meaningful portion of it was always earmarked for tax, and the SECURE Act framework simply determines how quickly and at whose marginal rate that portion gets paid. Running this same math against your own retirement account balances and your own children's approximate tax brackets is the single most useful exercise this section can offer — it turns an abstract awareness that "taxes will apply" into an actual number, which is the only version of this information specific enough to plan around.

8.3 What You Can Actually Do About It

None of the rules in the previous section can be waived or negotiated around after the fact. But the timing and structure of how your retirement accounts eventually get taxed is genuinely something you can influence while you're still alive and still making decisions, and this section covers the countermeasures worth understanding, roughly in order of how broadly they apply.

The most broadly useful strategy for many readers is a Roth conversion, executed deliberately during a specific window many people don't realize they have: the years between retirement and the point where required minimum distributions begin. During this window, income often drops meaningfully compared to peak working years, since salary has stopped but Social Security and mandatory account withdrawals haven't started yet, which can place a retiree temporarily in a lower tax bracket than they occupied for most of their working life, and often lower than their adult children currently occupy. Converting a portion of a traditional IRA to a Roth IRA during this window means paying ordinary income tax on the converted amount now, at this temporarily favorable rate, rather than leaving that same money to be withdrawn later by an heir who may be taxed at a considerably higher rate during their own peak earning years, exactly as illustrated in the previous section's example. Once converted, a Roth IRA grows tax-free, and critically, an inherited Roth IRA carries none of the required annual distributions during the ten-year window that apply to an inherited traditional account, since the original owner never had a required beginning date to trigger that requirement in the first place — meaning an heir inheriting a Roth can let the full balance continue growing tax-free for the entire ten years before needing to withdraw anything at all, and owes no income tax on any of it when they eventually do.

Executing this strategy well requires watching a specific trap that catches people who convert too aggressively in pursuit of tax savings: the Medicare IRMAA cliff. Income-Related Monthly Adjustment Amount surcharges increase Medicare Part B and Part D premiums once modified adjusted gross income crosses specific thresholds, and unlike ordinary tax brackets which increase gradually, these surcharges jump in discrete steps, meaning a conversion that pushes income just over a threshold can trigger a meaningfully higher Medicare premium for the following year, sometimes costing more in elevated premiums than the conversion saved in taxes. A well-built conversion schedule spreads the taxable event across several years specifically to stay below these thresholds each year, rather than converting a large amount in a single year and inadvertently triggering both a higher marginal tax bracket and an IRMAA surcharge simultaneously.

For readers with charitable intentions already part of their financial picture, qualified charitable distributions offer a genuinely efficient tool available starting at age seventy and a half. This provision allows a traditional IRA owner to direct funds straight from the IRA to a qualifying charity, and the amount transferred this way counts toward satisfying that year's required minimum distribution without being included in the owner's taxable income at all — a meaningfully better outcome than withdrawing the funds personally, paying tax on them, and then donating the after-tax amount and claiming a charitable deduction, since the qualified charitable distribution bypasses the income recognition entirely rather than offsetting it after the fact.

This charitable option connects to a broader beneficiary-selection strategy worth considering directly if your Distribution Intent statement from chapter two includes any charitable giving at all: naming a charity as the beneficiary of pre-tax retirement accounts specifically, while directing Roth accounts and other already-taxed assets to your children instead. A charity, as a tax-exempt entity, owes no income tax when it receives a traditional IRA or 401(k), meaning the full pre-tax balance reaches the charity with none of the deferred tax burden ever actually being paid by anyone. Your children, meanwhile, receive assets that either already carry a stepped-up basis or, in the case of a Roth account, generate no taxable income at all upon withdrawal. Structured this way, the same total estate value reaches your intended recipients with meaningfully less of it lost to tax overall, simply by matching each asset's tax character to the recipient best positioned to receive it efficiently.

Finally, for readers whose Distribution Intent statement calls for a trust to be the beneficiary of a retirement account, rather than an individual person — relevant for a beneficiary who is a minor, has special needs as covered in chapter nine, or simply shouldn't receive full and immediate control of a large account outright — a specific structural decision has to be made correctly, because getting it wrong can inadvertently trigger the least favorable tax treatment available. A conduit trust requires that any distribution the trust receives from the retirement account be passed straight through to the trust's beneficiary in that same year, which preserves the beneficiary's own life expectancy or ten-year timeline for tax purposes but offers little in the way of actual asset protection, since the funds pass straight through rather than being held. An accumulation trust, by contrast, allows the trustee to hold distributions inside the trust rather than passing them straight through, offering considerably more control and protection, but historically risked being taxed at the compressed and much higher trust income tax brackets rather than the beneficiary's own, more favorable individual rate, depending on how the trust and its distributions are structured. This is a decision with genuine complexity and real consequences for how much tax ultimately gets paid, and it's one of the clearest points in this entire book where the honest recommendation is not to attempt the drafting yourself, but to bring this specific question, along with your Distribution Intent statement, directly to an estate attorney experienced in retirement account trust structures.

Pulling these pieces together into something actionable, build a simple multi-year schedule sized to your own tax bracket: estimate your income in each year between retirement and the start of required minimum distributions, identify how much room exists in each year before crossing into a higher bracket or an IRMAA threshold, and convert a deliberate, consistent amount within that room each year rather than either ignoring the opportunity entirely or converting too aggressively in a single year. Paired with a beneficiary structure that sends pre-tax dollars where they'll be taxed least and already-taxed dollars where they'll be received most cleanly, this is the closest thing available to actually controlling a tax bill that, left alone, your heirs would otherwise inherit on the government's terms rather than yours.

Chapter 9 — Plan for Complicated Families and Businesses

Everything covered in this book so far has assumed, more or less, a family situation that fits neatly into the standard template: one marriage, shared children, a straightforward path from parent to child. Most estate planning materials, including most of the boilerplate documents and online templates available today, share that same assumption. The problem is that a meaningful share of the families reading this book don't actually fit it, and standard documents fail hardest, most expensively, and most personally destructively at exactly the points where real life diverges from that template. This chapter addresses the situations that standard planning handles worst: blended families, vulnerable beneficiaries, and business or cross-border complications. This section starts with the one that causes the most damage when it goes wrong, because it involves the people closest to you disagreeing about money at the exact moment they're also grieving.

Blended families — where one or both spouses have children from a previous relationship — sit at the center of more estate litigation than almost any other family structure, and the reason isn't usually malice. It's structural. A standard will, the kind covered in chapter three, that simply leaves everything to a surviving spouse assumes that spouse will eventually pass whatever remains along to all the children involved, including stepchildren from the other spouse's prior relationship, fairly and according to the deceased spouse's original wishes. This assumption fails more often than people expect, not always because the surviving spouse acts in bad faith, but because circumstances change, new relationships form, new wills get written, and a surviving spouse's own priorities naturally shift over years or decades of life continuing without their late partner. A parent who dies trusting that their spouse will eventually take care of that parent's own children from an earlier marriage has no actual legal mechanism ensuring that happens — only a hope, resting entirely on someone else's future decisions, made years later, under circumstances the deceased parent has no ability to influence or verify.

The tool built specifically to solve this problem is the qualified terminable interest property trust, introduced briefly in chapter four and worth returning to here with the full context that makes it relevant. A QTIP trust allows a first-to-die spouse to provide real, meaningful support for their surviving spouse during that spouse's remaining lifetime — income from the trust's assets, and in many structures the right to live in a shared home — while simultaneously guaranteeing, through the trust's own irrevocable terms rather than through a promise, that whatever principal remains in the trust when the surviving spouse eventually dies passes exactly where the first spouse specified, typically to that first spouse's own children from an earlier marriage. This resolves the core tension blended families face: the desire to genuinely provide for a second spouse without that provision quietly becoming a permanent disinheritance of children from an earlier relationship, dependent entirely on the second spouse's discretion and goodwill years down the road.

Remarriage after a spouse's death introduces a related risk worth naming directly, because it changes the calculation for anyone currently planning around a surviving spouse eventually remarrying. A surviving spouse who remarries may, intentionally or through the ordinary practical entanglement of building a new shared life, end up commingling inherited assets with a new spouse's assets, updating their own estate plan in ways that favor the new marriage, or simply losing track of an original intention to eventually pass remaining assets to stepchildren who are no longer part of daily life the way they once were. A properly structured QTIP trust, because its terms were locked in by the first spouse and can't be altered by the surviving spouse regardless of who they later marry, protects against exactly this scenario, which a simple will handing assets outright to a surviving spouse cannot.

For couples entering a second marriage, coordinating a prenuptial agreement with the broader estate plan is worth addressing directly rather than treating as a separate, unrelated legal matter handled by a different attorney with no communication between the two processes. A prenuptial agreement typically governs what happens to assets in the event of divorce, but many well-drafted agreements also address estate rights, specifically the elective share many states guarantee a surviving spouse regardless of what a will says — a legal protection that can override a spouse's stated wishes to leave the bulk of an estate to children from a prior marriage, unless that spousal right has been properly waived in advance through the prenuptial agreement itself. Estate planning documents and a prenuptial agreement drafted without reference to each other can end up working against one another, with the will attempting to accomplish something the elective share law still allows a spouse to override, defeating careful planning through a gap nobody thought to close.

The practical challenge underlying all of this is making unequal treatment among children defensible rather than explosive, and the difference between those two outcomes usually comes down to documentation, not to the underlying decision itself. Families regularly and reasonably choose unequal distributions for legitimate reasons — one child provided years of caregiving the others didn't, one child received significant financial help earlier in life that others didn't, one child has a demonstrated pattern of financial instability that makes an outright distribution unwise. The problem isn't the unequal decision. It's an unequal decision left unexplained, discovered cold by the children involved only after a parent's death, with no context, no explanation, and no opportunity to hear the reasoning directly from the parent who made it. Unexplained unequal treatment reads as favoritism or rejection, even when the actual reasoning was fair and considered. Documented, explained unequal treatment, ideally communicated directly while you're still alive rather than left to be discovered in a will, reads as a parent's honest judgment about a specific family's specific circumstances.

Consider a case that illustrates disinheritance handled correctly rather than carelessly. A father chose to leave a considerably smaller share to one of his three adult children, based on substantial financial support he'd already provided that child earlier in life, support the other two children had not received and had never asked for. Rather than simply writing an unequal residuary clause and leaving his children to discover it after his death with no explanation attached, he did two additional things while he was still alive and able to. He wrote a personal letter, kept with his estate planning documents rather than integrated into the legally operative will itself, explaining his reasoning plainly and without hostility — naming the specific financial support already provided, acknowledging it directly rather than pretending it hadn't happened, and stating clearly that his decision reflected fairness as he understood it, not any lesser regard for the child receiving less. And he had a direct conversation with all three of his children together, while he was healthy and the conversation could happen calmly, rather than leaving the topic to surface for the first time during a moment of grief. When he died years later, the will's unequal distribution matched exactly what his children already knew was coming, already understood the reasoning behind, and had already had the opportunity to discuss directly with their father while he was alive to answer questions. No litigation followed. No relationships fractured. The unequal share was identical to what an unexplained, undocumented version of the same decision would have specified — the difference was entirely in the documentation and the conversation surrounding it, not in the underlying distribution itself.

The throughline across every scenario in this section is the same: complicated family situations don't get resolved by hoping the people involved will eventually do the right thing on their own, whether that's a surviving spouse eventually providing for stepchildren, a remarried spouse remembering an earlier promise, or children quietly accepting an unequal share they were never given any context for. They get resolved by structures — a QTIP trust with terms that can't be altered later, a prenuptial agreement coordinated with the estate plan rather than drafted in isolation, a documented explanation paired with a direct conversation held while you're still able to have it. Trust in a future person's good judgment is not a plan. It's a hope standing in for one, and this section exists to help you replace it with something considerably more reliable.

9.2 Matching the Structure to the Person

The default instinct in most estate planning is to split everything evenly among children and call it fair. For many families, that instinct is entirely appropriate, and nothing in this section argues against it as a general starting point. But equal isn't always the same as protective, and this section addresses the beneficiaries whose circumstances mean an outright, unconditional inheritance could actually work against them rather than for them — not because they don't deserve the inheritance, but because the form it arrives in matters as much as the amount.

Start with minor children, a situation chapter six already touched on briefly but worth returning to with the full range of options available. Naming a minor directly as a beneficiary, as chapter six established, typically forces funds into court-supervised conservatorship until that child turns eighteen, followed by an unconditional lump-sum release at an age most parents wouldn't otherwise choose to hand a child significant, unsupervised money. A common alternative, the Uniform Transfers to Minors Act account, avoids the court supervision problem but still shares the second flaw: funds held in a UTMA account typically become the child's outright, unrestricted property at whatever age their state sets, commonly twenty-one, with no ability for a parent to extend that timeline or attach any conditions once the account is established. For most families with meaningful assets at stake, a trust structured specifically for the child offers considerably more control than either option: a trustee can be instructed to distribute funds for education, health, and general support during the child's minority and young adulthood, with principal released in stages, perhaps a portion at twenty-five, more at thirty, rather than the entire inheritance landing at once, at an age that may or may not correspond to actual readiness.

Special needs trusts address an entirely different problem, one where the stakes of getting the structure wrong are considerably higher than a matter of financial maturity. A beneficiary receiving means-tested government benefits, most commonly Supplemental Security Income or Medicaid, generally faces strict asset limits to maintain eligibility for those programs — often just a few thousand dollars in countable assets. An outright inheritance, even a modest one, can push that beneficiary over the threshold and disqualify them from benefits they depend on, sometimes benefits that took years to establish and that private funds could never fully replace, particularly ongoing medical coverage. A properly structured special needs trust holds the inheritance separately from the beneficiary's own countable assets, using trust funds to pay for things that supplement rather than replace government benefits — therapies, equipment, experiences, quality-of-life expenses the government program doesn't cover — while leaving the underlying benefit eligibility fully intact. The distinction between a first-party and third-party special needs trust matters considerably here: a first-party trust holds assets that belonged to the beneficiary themselves, such as a settlement or an inheritance already received outright before the structure was corrected, and typically requires a Medicaid payback provision upon the beneficiary's death, reimbursing the government for benefits provided during their lifetime. A third-party special needs trust, funded directly by a parent or other family member as part of estate planning rather than holding the beneficiary's own assets, carries no such payback requirement, which makes proactive planning during your lifetime meaningfully more advantageous than leaving a family to correct the structure reactively after an outright inheritance has already disqualified a loved one from benefits they needed.

A different category of beneficiary calls for a different kind of structure entirely: not a beneficiary who's vulnerable due to age or disability, but one whose current life circumstances make an outright inheritance genuinely risky, either to the beneficiary themselves or to the inheritance's ability to actually reach and benefit them as intended. A spendthrift trust addresses a beneficiary facing active addiction or a demonstrated pattern of poor financial judgment by restricting their direct access to trust principal, instead channeling distributions through a trustee's judgment, and by shielding the trust's assets from that beneficiary's own creditors, since assets the beneficiary never directly controls generally can't be reached by people or institutions the beneficiary owes money to. A discretionary trust extends this control further, giving the trustee genuine judgment over when and how much to distribute, rather than following a fixed, predictable schedule a creditor or a beneficiary in crisis could anticipate and plan around. And for a beneficiary in a marriage that feels genuinely unstable, structuring an inheritance so that it stays outside of marital property, held in trust rather than distributed outright into jointly titled accounts, can meaningfully protect the inheritance itself from being divided in a future divorce, an outcome many parents would prefer to avoid regardless of how they feel about the marriage itself.

An incentive trust takes a more targeted approach, tying distributions to specific milestones or behaviors the parent wants to encourage or discourage — releasing funds upon completion of a degree, matching a beneficiary's own earned income up to a certain amount, or withholding distributions during a period of documented substance abuse treatment. These structures require careful drafting to avoid becoming either toothless or unreasonably controlling from beyond the grave, and they work best when built around a genuine, specific understanding of the beneficiary's actual situation rather than a generic template borrowed from an unrelated family's circumstances.

The point underlying every structure in this section is the same: equal distribution and identical structure are two different decisions, and conflating them is where families go wrong. A parent can leave precisely equal dollar amounts to three children while structuring each inheritance completely differently — an outright distribution to one child with a stable, demonstrated track record, a staged trust for a younger child still establishing financial maturity, and a discretionary spendthrift structure for a third child facing circumstances that make an outright inheritance genuinely risky. None of this requires unequal amounts, and none of it requires explaining away favoritism the way section 9.1's unequal-shares discussion addressed. It simply requires looking honestly at each beneficiary as an individual person with a specific situation, rather than defaulting to identical structures because identical feels simpler or more obviously fair on the surface.

9.3 Businesses and Borders

The final complications this chapter addresses move outside the family relationships covered so far and into two areas that carry their own specialized rules: business ownership passing to the next generation, and estates that cross international lines, whether through a non-citizen spouse or property held in another country.

For anyone who owns an interest in a business alongside partners or co-owners, the single most important document determining what happens to that ownership interest at death often isn't the will or the trust at all — it's the buy-sell agreement, a contract among the business's owners specifying exactly what happens to an owner's interest when they die, become disabled, or otherwise exit the business. Without one in place, a deceased owner's interest typically passes according to their will or state default rules directly to their heirs, who may have no interest in or capability of actually running the business, creating an immediate and often contentious mismatch between the surviving business partners, who now have an unwilling or unqualified new co-owner, and the deceased owner's family, who may want cash rather than an illiquid ownership stake in a company they can't influence or easily sell. A well-drafted buy-sell agreement resolves this in advance by establishing a predetermined mechanism, often funded specifically by life insurance policies the business or the co-owners carry on each other, so that upon an owner's death, the remaining owners have both the contractual right and the actual cash, arriving immediately through the insurance payout, to buy out the deceased owner's interest at a fair, pre-agreed valuation, while the deceased owner's family receives cash rather than an ownership stake they'd have no practical way to use.

Beyond the buy-sell agreement itself, the business's operating agreement, if it's structured as an LLC, or its shareholder agreement, if it's a corporation, frequently contains its own transfer restrictions that operate independently of and sometimes in direct tension with whatever your personal estate planning documents say. Some operating agreements restrict ownership transfers to specific categories of people, require existing owners' approval before any transfer to an outside party takes effect, or trigger a mandatory buyout at a formula-based valuation regardless of what a will or trust attempts to specify. Chapter four's brief mention of assigning an LLC interest into a trust applies here with the same caution: the governing agreement's terms typically control, and estate planning documents drafted without direct reference to that agreement can end up conflicting with restrictions the business itself has already legally established.

Underlying all of this sits a decision worth making deliberately rather than by default: succession versus sale. Passing a business to the next generation only makes sense if that next generation genuinely wants to run it and has the capability to do so — an assumption worth testing honestly rather than simply assuming out of sentiment or habit, since a business handed to unwilling or unprepared heirs often loses value quickly, sometimes taking a family's other assets down with it if debts or obligations tied to the business remain unresolved. For families without a clear, willing, capable successor, planning proactively for an eventual sale, whether to an outside buyer, a co-owner, or key employees, and building that expectation directly into the estate plan rather than defaulting to automatic inheritance, often serves both the business's continued value and the family's actual financial interests considerably better than an unexamined assumption that passing it down is automatically the right choice.

Cross-border complications introduce a different category of specialized rules entirely, and two are worth flagging directly because they surprise people who don't expect international considerations to apply to what otherwise feels like an ordinary domestic estate. The unlimited marital deduction, which normally allows one spouse to leave any amount of assets to the other with no federal estate tax consequence regardless of size, does not apply if the surviving spouse is not a United States citizen. Without specific additional planning, a non-citizen spouse can face estate tax exposure on an inheritance that would have passed completely tax-free to a citizen spouse. The specific tool that restores similar protection is a qualified domestic trust, commonly called a QDOT, which holds the inheritance for the non-citizen spouse's benefit under specific IRS-mandated terms, deferring the estate tax until the QDOT itself eventually distributes principal, rather than triggering it immediately at the first spouse's death. Any couple where one spouse is not a United States citizen needs this addressed directly and specifically, since the standard assumption that everything simply passes to a spouse tax-free doesn't hold in this situation.

Property owned in another country introduces a separate complication, because that property is generally governed by the laws of the country where it sits, not by your American will or trust, regardless of how clearly your domestic documents state your intentions. Many countries, particularly across much of Europe and Latin America, apply forced-heirship rules, which mandate that a fixed portion of an estate must legally pass to specific relatives, typically children, regardless of what the deceased person's will says, overriding personal wishes in a way that would be unfamiliar to anyone used to the flexibility of American estate law. A vacation property, an inherited family home abroad, or any real estate held outside the United States needs to be addressed specifically with an attorney licensed in that particular country, since an American estate planning document generally has no authority to override that country's own succession laws.

For both the business and cross-border situations covered in this section, the honest advice is the same: these are precisely the areas where this book's role shifts from doing the planning yourself to identifying exactly which specialist to hire and arriving at that specialist's office already prepared. For business succession, that means a business succession attorney working alongside whoever handles the company's tax and valuation questions, brought in specifically to draft or review the buy-sell agreement against the operating agreement's existing terms. For a non-citizen spouse, that means an estate attorney experienced specifically in QDOT structures, not simply a general estate planning practice. For foreign property, that means an attorney licensed in the specific country where the property sits, coordinated with your domestic estate attorney rather than working in isolation from your broader plan. None of these situations are ones this book can fully resolve on its own, and knowing that clearly, along with knowing exactly which question to bring to which specialist, is itself the most useful outcome this section can offer.

Good — pricing confirmed. Writing the chapter now.

Chapter 10 — Build, Sign, and Maintain Your Plan

Nine chapters into this book, you've built an Estate Map, sorted probate from non-probate assets, written a Distribution Intent statement, and worked through the specific mechanics of wills, trusts, incapacity documents, beneficiary designations, taxes, retirement accounts, and whatever family or business complications apply to your situation. What's left is the part people tend to avoid even after doing all of that thinking: actually building the documents, signing them correctly, and keeping them current. This final chapter exists because knowledge that never turns into signed paperwork protects nobody, and because the objections that keep people stuck at this final step are almost always more assumption than fact.

Start with the four objections that show up most often, because each one deserves a direct answer rather than a dismissal.

"I'm not rich enough for this to matter" treats estate planning as something that exists primarily to manage large fortunes, when in fact the parts of this book that matter most to an ordinary household — a properly executed will, a durable power of attorney, a healthcare directive, aligned beneficiary forms — have nothing to do with wealth level at all. Chapter one's cost table applies just as forcefully to a five-hundred-thousand-dollar estate as it does to a five-million-dollar one; probate delays, guardianship risk, and beneficiary contradictions don't check your net worth before causing damage. If anything, a modest estate with less room for error and less ability to absorb legal fees and delays has more, not less, at stake in getting this right the first time.

"Trusts are only for wealthy people" confuses one specific tool with the entire discipline this book covers. Chapter four explained plainly that a revocable living trust's real value lies in probate avoidance, privacy, and incapacity management, none of which require significant wealth to matter — a modest estate still goes through the same court process, on largely the same timeline, as a large one, if it lacks a properly funded trust. Whether a trust is worth its cost for your specific situation is a fair question this book has already helped you answer honestly, but the answer isn't determined by a wealth threshold. It's determined by how much you value avoiding probate, how much privacy matters to you, and how prepared you want your family to be if incapacity arrives before death does.

"The software is fine" is sometimes true and sometimes a serious miscalculation, and the honest answer depends entirely on which category your situation falls into, a question this section addresses directly in a moment. What's worth challenging here is the assumption that the question has one universal answer. DIY software handles some situations well and handles others in a way that produces a document that looks complete while quietly failing to accomplish what you actually needed.

"My kids will sort it out" is the objection this entire book has been built to dismantle, chapter by chapter. Sorting it out is exactly what probate, guardianship proceedings, contradictory beneficiary forms, and unexplained unequal distributions make expensive, slow, and sometimes permanently damaging to family relationships. Your children sorting it out isn't a plan. It's the absence of one, dressed up as confidence in their competence.

With those objections addressed, here's how to actually decide among your three real paths forward, along with current, honest pricing for each. A do-it-yourself approach using reputable online software or templates typically costs remarkably little — a basic will can run under a hundred dollars, and even a DIY living trust template generally falls in the range of thirty to two hundred dollars. This path can produce a genuinely valid, legally sound set of documents for a straightforward situation: a single person or a first marriage with no unusual family structure, a modest and uncomplicated set of assets, and clear, uncontested wishes that don't require nuanced legal language to express. A flat-fee online service sits in the middle, generally running somewhere between one hundred fifty and fifteen hundred dollars for a trust-based package, often bundling a pour-over will, powers of attorney, and a healthcare directive together, with some attorney involvement in reviewing or customizing the documents rather than a fully DIY process. A traditional attorney-drafted plan costs more but delivers correspondingly more judgment and customization: a simple attorney-drafted will typically runs somewhere between four hundred and eight hundred dollars, a standard revocable living trust generally falls between fifteen hundred and three thousand dollars, and a complete plan for a couple, including trust, will, powers of attorney, and healthcare directives, commonly lands between twenty-five hundred and five thousand dollars for a standard situation, climbing higher, sometimes considerably higher, for estates with real complexity.

That word, complexity, is the actual dividing line, and it's worth naming the four specific situations where choosing DIY software over an attorney isn't simply a reasonable cost-saving choice but something closer to malpractice against your own family, given everything the rest of this book has explained about how badly these particular situations go wrong when handled with generic, one-size-fits-all language. The first is a blended family, where chapter nine's entire discussion of QTIP trusts, remarriage risk, and unequal shares requires legal judgment no template can replicate, since the standard language in most DIY tools assumes a single, uncomplicated marriage and simply has no mechanism for the nuance a blended family actually requires. The second is any estate approaching the federal or a relevant state estate tax threshold discussed in chapter seven, where the tax strategies involved require professional structuring to actually work as intended rather than accidentally triggering the exposure they were meant to avoid. The third is a beneficiary with special needs who depends on means-tested government benefits, where chapter nine's warning about disqualifying a vulnerable person from essential benefits through an improperly structured inheritance is not a hypothetical risk but a documented, common failure of generic estate planning tools that don't ask the right questions. And the fourth is business ownership of any real complexity, where chapter nine's discussion of buy-sell agreements and operating agreement transfer restrictions requires coordination between your estate documents and your business's own governing agreements, a level of cross-referencing no standalone template is built to handle.

Outside of these four situations, the decision genuinely comes down to your own comfort level, your budget, and how much you value the judgment and liability protection an attorney provides even for a straightforward estate. There's no universally correct answer here, only an informed one. What matters is choosing your path with a clear understanding of exactly what you're trading — cost against customization, speed against professional judgment, simplicity against the specific protections this book has spent nine chapters explaining. Whichever path you choose, the next section walks through exactly how to move from decision to signed, funded documents within the ninety-day window this book promised you from the very first page.

10.2 The Ninety-Day Calendar

Every chapter in this book has built toward a specific promise made in the introduction: a signed, funded, aligned estate plan within ninety days. This section is where that promise turns into an actual schedule, because the single most common way estate planning fails isn't bad advice or bad documents. It's a plan that never gets past the draft stage, sitting half-finished for years while life continues and circumstances keep changing underneath it. Draft documents protect nobody. Only executed ones do.

Break the ninety days into five distinct phases, and treat each one as a genuine milestone rather than an open-ended task that can quietly drift.

The first three to four weeks belong to drafting. Whether you've chosen DIY software, a flat-fee service, or a traditional attorney, this phase is where your Estate Map from chapter two and your Distribution Intent statement from that same chapter get translated into actual legal language — a will, trust documents if applicable, powers of attorney, and healthcare directives. Set a firm deadline for this phase rather than letting it expand indefinitely, since drafting is the stage most prone to endless revision, particularly if you're working through it independently rather than with an attorney driving the timeline for you.

Once drafts exist, the next week belongs to review, and this step matters more than people expect it to. Read every draft document specifically against your Distribution Intent statement, checking clause by clause whether the language actually accomplishes what you wrote down in chapter two, not what you vaguely remember discussing during the drafting process. This is also the moment to apply chapter three's clause-by-clause reading skills directly to your own documents: confirm the residuary clause matches your actual wishes, confirm per stirpes or per capita language reflects a deliberate choice rather than a default nobody discussed, confirm guardian and executor nominations name the people you'd currently choose rather than an earlier draft's placeholder. Catching a mismatch here, before signing, costs nothing beyond attention. Catching it after your family is already settling your estate costs considerably more.

With review complete, move to execution, and treat this step with the precision chapter three's discussion of witness and notarization requirements described. Confirm your specific state's requirements for witnesses and notarization before the signing itself, gather witnesses who are not beneficiaries under the will, and complete a self-proving affidavit with a notary present wherever your state allows one. This is not a step to rush through casually at a kitchen table between other errands. A will or trust signed without meeting your state's exact formal requirements can be challenged or rejected outright, which means every other chapter's careful work collapses at the one procedural step that should have been the simplest.

The fourth phase, typically requiring two to four weeks depending on how many institutions are involved, is where chapter four's funding checklist and chapter six's beneficiary audit finally get executed rather than simply understood. Retitle real estate by preparing and recording new deeds wherever a trust requires it. Contact every bank and brokerage firm individually to retitle or transfer accounts into the trust's name. Submit updated beneficiary designation forms to every retirement account and life insurance policy custodian, correcting exactly the contradictions your chapter six audit identified. This phase is tedious by nature, involving repeated calls and forms across multiple institutions, and it's exactly the phase people abandon partway through, leaving a trust technically signed but functionally unfunded in precisely the way chapter four's twelve-hundred-dollar case file described.

Because that risk is so real and so common, build in a fifth and final phase that most plans skip entirely: confirmation in writing. For every account you retitled or every beneficiary form you submitted, request written confirmation back from the institution showing the change actually took effect, rather than assuming a form you mailed or submitted online was processed correctly. Financial institutions make administrative errors, forms get lost, and the only way to know your funding actually worked is to see it confirmed in writing, not to trust that submitting the paperwork was the same thing as completing the process.

Three additional pieces belong alongside the core legal documents, not because they carry the same formal legal weight, but because they determine whether your family can actually execute the plan you've built when the time comes. A letter of instruction, distinct from the will itself and not a legally binding document, should plainly list practical information your executor and family will need immediately: account numbers, the location of insurance policies, contact information for your attorney and financial advisor, and any specific wishes about matters too personal or too fluid to belong in a formal legal document, such as funeral preferences. A document location record should state plainly and specifically where each original signed document physically lives, since a perfectly executed will nobody can find functions, in practice, identically to no will at all. And a digital access record, increasingly essential and still frequently overlooked, should list how your executor or agent can access your digital accounts, email, and any online financial platforms, since modern estates increasingly include assets and information that exist nowhere on paper at all.

10.3 Keeping It Current

A signed, funded, aligned plan is not a permanent state. It's a snapshot of your life and your wishes at one particular moment, and it begins drifting out of accuracy the moment any part of that life changes. This final section installs the maintenance habit that keeps your plan from becoming, years from now, the same kind of stale document chapter one warned against.

Set a standing review on a three-year cycle, regardless of whether anything in your life feels like it's changed. Put an actual date on your calendar, not a vague intention to "look at this again sometime," and treat that date the way you'd treat any other recurring commitment with real consequences attached. During each review, pull out your Estate Map, your Distribution Intent statement, and the alignment audit from chapter six, and rerun the same conflict check you ran when you first built this plan. Laws shift, account custodians change, and even a life that feels stable on the surface can accumulate small drift over three years that's worth catching before it compounds.

Beyond that standing three-year cycle, seven specific trigger events should prompt an immediate review, regardless of where you sit in that cycle. Marriage or remarriage changes nearly everything covered in this book, from beneficiary designations to the blended-family considerations in chapter nine. Divorce demands immediate attention to every beneficiary form and every fiduciary nomination, since an ex-spouse left in place on a retirement account or as an executor is exactly the failure pattern this book opened with. The birth of a child or grandchild often prompts a guardian nomination that didn't exist before, or a shift in how a trust's distribution terms should account for a new family member. A death in the family, whether of a beneficiary, an executor, or a named fiduciary, leaves a gap in your documents that needs filling before it's discovered by default during an actual estate settlement. A move to a different state matters because, as chapter three and chapter seven both explained, execution requirements and state estate tax exposure vary meaningfully by jurisdiction, and documents valid where they were signed don't automatically reflect the new state's specific rules or thresholds. The sale of a business changes or eliminates entirely the buy-sell and succession planning chapter nine described, since a document built around a business you no longer own no longer serves any purpose. And a major change in tax law, of exactly the kind chapter seven described happening to the federal exemption in recent years, can shift which strategies actually apply to your situation, sometimes dramatically, even if nothing in your own family circumstances has changed at all.

The last piece of maintenance isn't a document or a deadline. It's a conversation, and it's the one most families skip entirely, usually out of discomfort rather than any real barrier. Your adult children don't need to know dollar figures if you'd rather keep that private, and there's nothing wrong with holding that boundary. What they do need to know is that a plan exists, roughly where it's kept, who to contact, and why any unequal or unusual structures were chosen, following exactly the model chapter nine's case file demonstrated. A workable version of that conversation can start simply: telling them you've completed your estate planning and that the documents are stored in a specific, named location, along with your attorney's or advisor's contact information. Letting them know who's been named executor, trustee, or healthcare agent, and briefly why, so nobody is surprised or confused when that person needs to act. And if any part of the plan involves unequal treatment or an unusual structure, whether a special needs trust, a QTIP arrangement, or simply an uneven distribution, explaining the reasoning in plain terms, the same way the father in chapter nine's case file did, so the plan is understood and accepted well before it's ever actually needed. This conversation doesn't require a single sitting or a formal announcement. It can happen gradually, over several conversations, at whatever pace feels comfortable. What matters is that it happens at all, while you're still here to have it — because a plan your family understands and trusts settles an estate in weeks. A plan they discover cold, with no context and no warning, is where every failure this book opened with actually begins.

Conclusion: Your Ninety-Day Plan Starts Now

Ten chapters ago, this book opened with a woman standing in a hallway, holding a will that had cost her husband three hundred dollars and controlling almost none of what he actually owned. It's worth closing with the same picture, because everything in between was built to change how that story ends, and now is the moment to see the whole shape of what you've actually built rather than the individual pieces you worked through one chapter at a time.

Strip away all the terminology, all the clause names and account types and tax thresholds, and what remains is genuinely simple: four systems, one map connecting them, and zero contradictions between what any of them say. The will handles what's left over after everything else has been accounted for. The trust, if you have one, handles what's actually been funded into it, and only what's been funded into it. The incapacity documents handle the years, sometimes many years, when you're alive but unable to act for yourself. And the beneficiary designations and titling, quietly controlling more of your actual wealth than most people ever realize, handle everything that passes by contract rather than by will. Four systems, each with its own job, each needing to say the same thing the others say. That's the entire architecture. Everything from the Estate Map in chapter two to the alignment audit in chapter six existed to build and then verify that single structure.

Set against that structure is a choice worth naming plainly, because it's the actual decision underneath everything this book has walked you through. On one side sits the cost of misalignment: years spent in probate that a funded trust would have avoided entirely, tens of thousands of dollars in fees and delay that a few properly retitled accounts would have prevented, and in the worst cases, a family fractured over a contradiction nobody meant to create and nobody caught in time. That's not a hypothetical cost. It's the cost Tom's family paid, and it's the cost this entire book has been built to help you avoid. On the other side sits the actual price of doing this work: a few weekends of focused attention, spread across the ninety-day calendar chapter ten laid out, and a fee you know in advance, whether that's the cost of software, a flat-fee service, or an attorney's quoted price. Stated side by side like that, the trade barely qualifies as a difficult decision. It only feels difficult beforehand, when the work is still abstract and the cost of skipping it hasn't yet come due.

So here is the one thing this book is actually asking you to do, and it's deliberately not a list. Go back to the twelve-question audit at the end of chapter one, find whichever item scored as your highest-risk red flag, and finish it this week. For a meaningful share of readers, that item will turn out to be a single beneficiary form, sitting on a retirement account you haven't checked in years, and correcting it will take a phone call and about eleven minutes of your time. That's not a small thing pretending to be a big one. Chapter six spent real space explaining exactly why that one form can override every other document you own, exactly as it did for Tom's family. Fixing it isn't a token gesture. For some readers, it will be the single most consequential eleven minutes of financial protection they take all year. What matters right now isn't finishing everything this book covered. It's not letting today end without having moved, even slightly, on the item that matters most. Momentum carries a plan forward. Comprehensiveness, chased too early, is usually just another reason to wait.

When you're ready to keep building past that first step, the appendices at the back of this book are built to support exactly the ninety-day process chapter ten described. State-by-state tables lay out probate timelines and estate tax thresholds so you're not guessing at figures that vary by jurisdiction. The funding checklist from chapter four is reproduced in full, organized by asset type, ready to work through account by account. Twelve specific questions for interviewing an attorney give you a way to walk into that meeting prepared rather than starting from nothing. And a letter of instruction template turns chapter ten's advice about practical, non-legal information into an actual document you can fill in this weekend.

Picture, once more, the woman from the introduction, and picture her story told differently. Same assets. Same family. But this time, every account matches every document, every beneficiary form was checked and corrected years before it was ever needed, and when the time came, her family settled everything in about six weeks, paying nothing beyond the flat fee they'd agreed to at the very start. No surprises. No litigation. No second wife nobody remembered to remove from a form. Just a plan that said the same thing everywhere it was asked, built by someone who read this book, found their highest-risk item, and started this week instead of someday. That's not a better story because it's less real. It's better because it's still entirely available to you, starting now.

www.ingramcontent.com/pod-product-compliance
Lightning Source LLC
LaVergne TN
LVHW050825061126
851857LV00012B/982